Infant-Toddler Social Studies

Infant-Toddler Social Studies

Activities to Develop a Sense of Self

Carla B. Goble, PhD

Redleaf Press®
www.redleafpress.org
800-423-8309

Published by Redleaf Press
10 Yorkton Court
St. Paul, MN 55117
www.redleafpress.org

First edition 2017
Cover design by Mayfly Design
Cover photograph by logoboom/Shutterstock.com
Interior design by Mayfly Design
Typeset in the Arno Pro and Archer
Printed in the United States of America
24 23 22 21 20 19 18 17   1 2 3 4 5 6 7 8

Library of Congress Cataloging-in-Publication Data
CIP data has been applied for

Printed on acid-free paper

This book is dedicated to my children and grandchildren, who have each enriched my life in countless ways, and to all children and the families and caregivers who nurture, teach, and encourage them to learn about themselves and the world.

Contents

· ·

Acknowledgments

· ·

I want to acknowledge the editors and staff of Redleaf Press who have supported and guided this effort. Their knowledge, skills, and ongoing assistance in the writing of this book are greatly appreciated. I would also like to acknowledge John C. McCullers, who was my child development professor at Oklahoma State University. His high expectations and depth of child development knowledge, as well as his encouragement, changed the trajectory of my professional life. It was his teaching that made this book possible.

Introduction

. . . .

When I first became an infant teacher, I began to think about how my interactions and the learning opportunities I provided affected the babies in my care. I noticed that the way I interacted with them influenced how the babies felt about themselves, how they felt about me and other people, and how they interacted with the world around them. It was sobering to realize how much influence my caregiving and teaching had. I suspect you think about these things too as you care for the infants and toddlers in your program.

Identifying how and why we do things and how our interactions affect infant and toddler development and well-being was of utmost importance in my thoughts and my work. I focused on how to help babies grow and develop into children who feel capable and positive about themselves, who respect and know how to get along with others, and who feel connected as contributing members of their communities—all social-studies skills. Although the development of these skills takes a lifetime, the foundation for these capabilities is built during the infant and toddler years.

I wrote this book to highlight the importance of providing social-studies learning experiences and opportunities for infants and toddlers. It is meant to be a resource for you in planning interactions that support development of a positive sense of self and an ability to relate to and interact with others and the environment. It is full of activities, presented in a developmental progression, designed to help infants and toddlers build on each previous social-studies learning experience. Although the activities are organized by age, I encourage you to reflect on each child's individual rate of development as well as the social-emotional needs of the whole group as you are planning activities. Each learning experience is designed to help promote young children's development of healthy relationships, prosocial skills, community connectedness, feelings of competence, and pride in their families and home cultures.

Content

This book begins by defining what social-studies learning looks like in an early childhood program. The first chapter focuses on the importance of providing social-studies learning opportunities for infants and toddlers in ways that are developmentally appropriate and that meet the emotional needs of the age group. Young children develop a variety of skills in their early years that can be categorized into domains. Development of the whole child looks at how those skills are interconnected.

For example, a child's motor-skill development can affect his ability to explore and interact with others, objects, or the environment. When toddlers begin to walk upright, it frees their hands to explore and changes their perspective. No longer are they lying on their backs or stomachs or crawling on the floor. When they are walking, toddlers can easily move across the room and see things at eye level on shelves or low tables. New capabilities bring about new ways of learning and signal to caregivers the need for adaptations to the learning environment. In this case, you may put safe toys and objects on low shelves and tables for the children to handle so they can advance their motor-skill development and their growing independence and autonomy.

When you take the time to think about the whole child and how each area of development affects the others, you will be able to plan developmentally appropriate learning experiences and interactions for your program. Chapter 1 also includes a brief overview of child development and temperament. This information will help you think about how to individualize the caregiving and learning experiences you provide.

The richness of diversity in today's classrooms supports the opportunity for social-studies programming to help better prepare young children to understand themselves and others. Chapter 2, along with the activities in the following chapters, highlights the role of infant-toddler family involvement, the inclusion of home culture and language, and the building of partnerships between caregivers and families.

Chapter 3 is about you, the teacher or early childhood provider. It highlights the significant role you play in providing high-quality, developmentally appropriate programming and activities for young children. This chapter reviews professional guidelines and early learning standards. It also includes information on infant and toddler behavior cues that show children's readiness to learn. These cues can help you be aware of opportune times to interact with the infants and toddlers in your program, as well as help you notice and be aware of what they are capable of doing during different stages and levels of development. By recognizing these cues, you will be able to provide learning opportunities that support what children can currently do and provide achievable challenges that help them advance to the next level.

The remaining chapters, 4 through 9, include more than one hundred social-studies learning activities and interactions for infants and toddlers. The chapters are divided by age, beginning with infants from birth to four months. In chapter 4, learning activities address infants' needs for secure, trustful relationships and environments, supportive caregiving, and opportunities to begin learning about themselves. Each of the following chapters builds on the one before, helping you to provide learning opportunities that extend prior social-studies learning to more developmentally advanced understandings, skills, and behaviors.

How to Use This Book

Read the first three chapters of this book to learn about a developmental approach to social studies for infants and toddlers, the importance of family and culture in social-studies learning, and the critical role you play as a caregiver. Use chapters 4 through 9 to plan social-studies activities for your classroom. The activities are organized chronologically from birth to thirty-six months. The chapter age groups are as follows:

- Birth to 4 Months

- 4–8 Months

- 8–12 Months

- 12–18 Months

- 18–24 Months

- Two-Year-Olds

When choosing activities to use with the children in your care, it is important you understand how each activity chapter is organized. There are three social-studies developmental themes or categories for the activities in each chapter. Each of the themes is further broken down into areas of infant-toddler development. These are the developmental themes and areas:

1. Learning about oneself

    > sense of self
    > family

2. Learning to relate to and interact with other people

> social skills
> communication

3. Learning to relate to and interact with the environment

> classroom community
> broader community and society

Below is an outline of how each activity is presented.

Activity Title

Area

Developmental Objectives

Instructions

Extensions/Modifications

I recommend that you use all of the activities for each age group and repeat them daily over a period of time. Infants and toddlers learn best through repetition. Because each child develops at her own pace, you may use an activity from another chapter for a specific child. For example, sixteen-month-old Ari may be developmentally ready for an activity from chapter 8, which is typically used for children age eighteen to twenty-four months. You may decide to use activities written for a younger developmental level if a child or several children in your group need learning opportunities to develop skills that they have not previously had an opportunity to master.

There are forms and resources online to help you observe, reflect, and plan for the infants and toddlers in your group. Go to www.redleafpressorg/itss and click on the Web Components tab. These resources include a link to an online temperament assessment. This assessment provides suggestions for modifications to your environment and interactions based on its analysis of your temperament as well as each child's.

You'll also find checklists for infant-toddler development at www.redleafpress .org/itss. You can use the checklists to think about the developmental capabilities of each child in your classroom and to determine which of the social-studies activities in this book to use. The observation forms can be used with the activities to document infant-toddler learning behaviors and to help inform your future social-studies planning. These forms are designed to be used with an individual child or with several children.

To support you, the infant-toddler caregiver, there are also infant-toddler teacher self-assessments and a caregiver professional development plan available at www.redleafpress.org/itss. These resources are designed to help you build advanced knowledge and skills through self-assessment and self-determined professional development planning. I recommend that you complete the self-assessments every three to six months and plan, schedule, and complete professional development activities during the time between assessments. Using this time frame will not only help you acquire more advanced knowledge and skills but will also create a record of ongoing professional development.

It is with sincere recognition and gratitude for the important work that you do with infants, toddlers, and families that I have written this book. I know that your efforts benefit not only the children and families in your care but also our communities and society as a whole. My admiration for the care and teaching that you provide every day to young children is woven into the fabric of this book. I hope that you find the social-studies activities beneficial to your program and that each child in your care develops to his full capabilities through their use. I wish you the best as you continue to develop your infant-toddler professional knowledge and skills over the course of your career.

CHAPTER 1

Infant-Toddler Social Studies

· ·

Social studies focuses on understandings of people and how they relate to and interact with one another and the environment. Social studies for infants and toddlers is defined around three major developmental themes. These themes include learning about oneself, interacting with other people, and interacting with the environment. Each of the three themes can be broken down into two smaller areas of developmental focus.

The first theme is learning about oneself and being a family member. The two developmental areas of this theme focus on developing a sense of self and belonging to a family. Social-studies planning for this theme could include interactions that support each child's self-awareness: activities such as holding an infant in front of a mirror and talking with her about what she sees. To develop a sense of family belonging, have photographs of children's family members displayed where they can see them. This helps young children develop attachment to their families.

The second theme is learning to relate to and interact with other people. This theme's two developmental areas of focus are learning to communicate and developing social skills. Singing songs and talking to infants and toddlers are examples of social-studies learning activities for this theme. You could also model for an infant how to be near another baby or model for a toddler how to play with similar toys next to a friend.

The third theme is learning how to relate to and interact with the environment. The developmental areas included in this theme are interacting in the classroom community and interacting with the broader community and society. Teaching children the names of other children and teachers in the classroom and taking infants and toddlers on walks around the building and neighborhood are ways to provide social-studies interactions within this theme.

Activities and experiences that provide children opportunities to understand themselves and to relate to other people and the environment are the basis for social-studies learning in an infant-toddler program.

Understanding oneself, feeling good about oneself and one's capabilities, being able to form personal relationships, and being able to interact effectively with others begins at birth and continues over a lifetime. Social-studies learning opportunities for young children during the first three years of life can set the stage for later, more advanced skill development. When toddlers learn words to express how they feel and skills to self-regulate, they are better able to get along with other children in preschool or kindergarten and are able to focus and attend to learning tasks.

As infants become toddlers, their expanding senses of self and growing motor, language, and cognitive skills provide increasing opportunities for learning about the physical and social world around them. When toddlers begin to talk, they want to learn the names of things. They also begin to ask questions and want to know about other people, how things work, and what you can do with objects. This is an opportune time for you to teach words for feelings and to model for children how to express themselves and have social conversations with others.

Since infants and toddlers begin to experience and internalize the social norms, values, customs, and beliefs of their primary caregivers, supporting their home cultures and the development of a positive cultural identity is a vital component of social-studies learning for this age group. Including objects, music, and photographs in the classroom that reflect the ethnicities and cultures of the children's families helps them to develop a positive sense of self. In addition, providing infants and toddlers with extended and enriched interactions with the social world helps them begin to understand both themselves and others. Playing games with two or more children or having dolls with different skin tones and hair textures can help them to begin to connect with others. Within the early care program, children should be given opportunities to meet new and different kinds of people and to explore a variety of materials and environments.

A Professional Approach

National, state, and local education systems, communities, and policy makers have become increasingly aware of how important high-quality care and early experiences are for young children: High-quality infant-toddler programming provides supportive interactions and developmentally appropriate learning experiences to promote and enhance young children's development. You can use professional learning standards, professional ethics, child development theories, and developmentally appropriate practice as tools to help guide high-quality teaching practices and program policies.

Having a well-planned and implemented social-studies approach that includes developmentally appropriate activities and interactions is one component of high-quality infant-toddler programming. Use the activities in this book to guide your planning for social-studies learning experiences. For example, include music and musical instruments in the classroom from a variety of cultures, especially those of the children's families and home cultures. This specific social-studies activity supports infants' and toddlers' development of a positive sense of self, links them to their families and cultures, and provides opportunities for social interactions.

Child Development

Child development theories or explanations of how development occurs in young children are important considerations in the creation of high-quality infant-toddler programming. Theories of development and how it happens are often used in early childhood education to inform and determine how to care for, teach, and interact with infants and toddlers in ways that support their learning and development.

Understanding child development is critical to providing developmentally appropriate learning experiences for all children. Knowing what an infant or toddler can typically do at different stages and ages helps you plan social-studies interactions and learning experiences that support and advance children's development. Although child development focuses on the whole child, we often talk about it by domain or area. These domains are physical, social-emotional, communication/language, cognitive, and approaches to learning. Child development is predictable and occurs in a pattern. A typically developing infant first learns to hold up his head, then to roll over, later to sit alone, and even later to crawl and then walk. This illustrates a predictable pattern of physical development that most babies will go through.

As an infant-toddler teacher, you have probably noticed that although development is predictable and sequential, each child has her own individual rate of development, temperament characteristics, and approaches to learning. In any infant-toddler classroom, there is a broad range of individual developmental differences in children who are the same age. This is because each child's individual heredity, environment, and temperament traits influence development. Culture, child-rearing practices, and the values and goals of families and society are another set of influences that affect children's development. Because of this variety of development, including and partnering with families is an important component of planning infant-toddler social-studies interactions, activities, and learning experiences.

Individual temperament, differences in behavioral styles, emotional expression, and ways of responding to the environment affect how adults care for infants and toddlers. These responses affect the formation of caregiver-child relationships and influence children's development over time. Relationships between young children and adults are built through consistent, warm, responsive, and nurturing care. The types of relationships that infants and toddlers form with caregivers depends on how well the adults who care for them understand them and how those adults respond to and act toward them. The development of relationships is the foundation of social-studies learning for infants and toddlers and is vital to their well-being. These first relationships affect infants' and toddlers' ongoing development and their future capability to form healthy relationships.

Temperament

Teaching social studies to infants and toddlers focuses on the development of a positive sense of self, self-regulation skills, individual awareness, and effective self-coping strategies. Understanding that each child is an individual is an important component to helping children develop a positive sense of self. Babies are born with inherited temperament characteristics that influence how physically active they are, how they react to the environment and new experiences, and how strongly they express their emotions.

Temperament characteristics are also influenced by the child's culture and his family's expectations. As a caregiver, you should talk with families and observe each child to learn about his individual temperament characteristics. This can guide you in the planning and modifications that need to be made to best support their development and learning. You can be intentional in actively modifying your responses and interactions and the environment, and you can help infants and toddlers learn about themselves and provide experiences that help them develop self-regulation and self-awareness. For example, some children like to watch and are more cautious about new people and new things. They may not be as physically active as some other children and may become easily upset or frightened when something unexpected happens. They may cry more loudly and take longer to soothe themselves. A child with these temperament traits benefits when she has new experiences and people introduced to her slowly so she can get used to them. These children may need you to hold them more often, to reassure them, and to help them learn how to soothe themselves by giving them a comfort object such as a soft toy. These types of thoughtful and respectful teaching approaches allow you to support each child. As children grow and develop, the modifications, teaching strategies, and interactions you use to respond to individual temperament characteristics will change in response to each child's advancing development, learned skills, and ability to self-regulate.

Self-reflection is a skill that helps people modify and adapt their own behavior. When you make modifications in response to a child's temperament traits, you can help him develop a positive sense of self and learn strategies that help him regulate his own behavior. For example, a child whose temperament means that it takes time for him to get used to new people and new places needs a caregiver who respects these characteristics and adjusts the way that she interacts with the child. The caregiver can talk softly and reassure the child by telling him what she is going to do and what is going to happen. This helps the child feel more secure and gives him a chance to self-regulate and anticipate what will happen next. Information about the *Infant Toddler Temperament Tool (IT3)*, an interactive website designed to help you learn more about your own temperament characteristics as well as the characteristics for each child in your care, can be found online at www.ecmhc.org/temperament. This website also provides ideas for modifying your interactions with infants and toddlers, as well as the environment, based on your results.

Developmental Approach

Developmentally appropriate practice means knowing what the typical age-related capabilities of a group of children are and then using that knowledge to plan learning experiences. It also means observing and planning for all children's individual rates of development, combinations of temperaments, cultures, families, home languages, and other specific needs and characteristics.

The wonderful diversity of personalities, cultures, and families found in an infant-toddler classroom provides a rich environment and robust opportunity for social-studies learning. Children in infant and toddler classrooms exhibit a wide range of physical characteristics, behaviors, and developmental rates. To plan developmentally for a group of infants and toddlers means that you should consider the uniqueness of each child in the group. Conduct observations, reflect on what you know, and consider the group of children, the individuals within the group, and their families and cultures to plan developmentally appropriate learning experiences for the children in your care.

Materials on the Web Component tab include developmental checklists to help inform your planning for each child. You can use the checklists to reflect on the development of the children in your care and determine how to best support their learning and development. Your knowledge of each's child developmental level should guide your use of the social-studies activities in this book. Although the social-studies activities in chapters 4 through 9 are organized by chronological age groupings, children's actual development varies, and you may select activities from a variety of chapters, depending on the needs of an individual child or group of children.

CHAPTER 2

Infants, Toddlers, and Families

• •

Each child in your infant or toddler group is different and displays a mix of temperament traits that can be distinguished early in life. The family that each child is a part of is also unique. Families are made up of different configurations, races, ethnicities, beliefs, cultures, and experiences, among other things. As a caregiver, you must recognize that your relationships are also influenced by your own experiences, background, culture, and approach to work. Since the infant-toddler classroom is a blend of many different people and cultures, it provides a rich environment for learning social studies. Partnering with families and the community supports the development of infants and toddlers and is an important component of social-studies planning and teaching.

Culture

A person's culture is her way of life, and it includes customs, language, values, attitudes, and beliefs. Customs can include holidays, rituals, clothing, food, art, literature, and traditions. Cultural practices are learned and passed from one generation to the next within families and communities. Both verbal and nonverbal language, such as facial expressions, eye contact, and amounts of silence versus speaking, are also cultural. All cultural groups have value and bring dignity and rich diversity to society as a whole and to early childhood classrooms. It is important to keep in mind as you plan for infant and toddler social-studies experiences in your program that the values, assumptions, and perceptions a person has are culturally influenced.

Infants and Toddlers

Infants' and toddlers' cultures are defined by their families' daily practices and routines and influence their behaviors and how they learn. Infants and toddlers learn about themselves, others, and the world around them through the experiences and interactions they have with other people and the environment. They actively construct knowledge through their senses and through play. They like to explore and experiment, put things in their mouths, hold things in their hands, bang on objects, drop things, and figure out what they can do with their bodies. A child's exploration of her environment and her interactions with other people are the most powerful influences on what she will learn (Bronfenbrenner 1979, 1994; Bronfenbrenner and Morris 1998).

Infants' and toddlers' physical, social-emotional, language-communication, and cognitive development are ongoing. Although development is often described using domains or areas, teaching infants and toddlers requires thinking of the whole child and being aware that learning in one domain affects change in other areas. For example, when Adam learned how to sit without assistance, he no longer needed to support his body with his hands and arms. Now Adam can reach out for things, bat at objects, and pick up a toy. He can bring the toy to his face, look at it, and explore how it feels. When Adam developed this new skill in one area, the skill had an impact on other areas of his development. That interconnection is why the whole-child approach should be considered when planning learning experiences for infants and toddlers. Although the focus of this book is on social studies (primarily social and emotional areas of development), you should give insightful attention to all areas of development.

Infants and toddlers learn through repetition. They may have a particular song they like to listen to, and they may often choose the same book to read over and over again. The repetitive experiences and interactions they have on a daily basis strengthen the neural pathways they are forming. The formation of these pathways has a large impact on young children's future learning and development. The first three years of a child's life provide an opportunity to help facilitate optimal development in all domains and to build a strong social-studies foundation. When choosing activities from this book, keep in mind that repetition is important, and you should repeat activities over time.

Families

Families are groups of people made up of different ages, experiences, and stages of the human life span. Within a family, there are expectations of each member, including how they interact with one another and what roles they play. Each person affects everyone else in the family, including infants and toddlers. When a new baby is born or adopted, a member is added to the family system, and family members must make adaptations to the existing family structure. When a child enters group care for the first time, both the child and her family must adjust to the new situation. As a caregiver, you have far-reaching effects and a serious responsibility to infants and toddlers, their families, and the community. How you nurture and care for a child affects not only the child but also everyone else in that child's family.

A family system can be made up of people who may or may not be biologically related to one another. Family can be defined in legal terms, which means that you need to know who has the legal authority to make decisions about the children in your care as well as who has the legal right to have access to a child. But in nonlegal terms, families can include single parents; stepsiblings; grandparents raising grandchildren; and lesbian, gay, bisexual, or transgender parents, among many other configurations. As a family unit blends and changes, it forms a new group or system. A meaningful way to think of family is as a unit of emotionally bonded people who interact with and are interdependent on one another. Families typically share resources, values, living space, and goals. Thinking about families in this way is nonexclusionary and embraces the many different types of families you may find in your program. It also places the focus on the relationships among individual members and how they support and interact with one another. This flexible way of defining family allows you to best understand and support the families and children in your care. The blend of many different family configurations, people, and cultures provides a rich environment for infant-toddler social-studies learning.

Family Culture

Helping children develop a positive cultural identity is an important aspect of teaching infant and toddler social studies. Young children learn what language to speak, what foods to eat, and other cultural norms from their families and communities. The growing richness of diversity of young children in today's classrooms provides opportunities for you to learn about other cultures and to build new understandings that support the optimal development of all young children.

To effectively teach, you must understand, respect, and be comfortable with each family's culture—including language, approaches to infant care, food and eating preferences, sleeping arrangements, and attitudes about potty training, play, and learning. To understand these factors, you must first determine what they are. Two families that speak the same language may have other cultural characteristics that are different.

The roles of individuals within a family and the family's communication patterns are important for you to consider. Each family has physical and psychological boundaries and expectations that guide how they interact and behave with both their children and with you, the caregiver. Since beliefs about child development are shaped by cultural attitudes and cultural differences, social-studies programming requires an understanding, respect, and inclusion of different cultures.

A young child's development of self and his identity is inseparable from his family's social and cultural environment. Infants and toddlers tune in to the culture, customs, language, behaviors, beliefs, rituals, and activities of their family. During the first three years, they begin to learn language, form close relationships, and learn the traditions, cultural values, and practices of their families. Infants and toddlers also learn what behavior is expected of them in and out of the home and how to relate to others within their family and in the broader community. For children who are dual-language learners, their home language is linked to their culture and their ethnic identity. A strong emphasis is given to the use of home language and culture in the social-studies activities presented later in this book. Supporting a child's ability to speak her home language ensures a connectedness to her family and culture. The inability to communicate with family members breaks the bond to a child's family history, culture, and the formation of relationships.

For families whose primary language is not English, using their home language as much as possible with their children is critical to preserving the family's ethnic identity. From birth, babies respond to the sound of their families' voices. They hear their families' language and music, and as they grow, they begin to try to mimic and make the same sounds. As a caregiver, you should intentionally support home language for the children in your program. This will build their ability to maintain their family relationships and pride in their cultural heritage.

Some immigrant families may think that their children should learn and speak only the language of the new country. You can help families understand the benefits of their children learning both their home language as well as the language of the new country. Being a dual-language learner will help the children retain their connections to family and will also help them be successful in school and in society. You may not know all of the languages of the children who are in your care. However, you can learn how to support each child's ability to speak his home language through teaching and care practices that include home languages and by partnering with families to provide dual-language learning opportunities. The activities found later in this book will give you ways to include children's home languages. One example is the activity What My Family Eats for toddlers eighteen to twenty-four months, found on pages 121–122.

Infant-Toddler Social Studies and Family Culture

Social studies for infants and toddlers begins with their families. When you partner with families, you can effectively provide young children with more engaging, relevant learning content that will support their development. Each child's family, ethnicity, language, and culture are primary components of your social-studies planning and teaching. The activities in this book emphasize the involvement of families and the inclusion of cultural content that is directly linked to children's homes. Embedding home culture into social-studies content for infants and toddlers as well as forming strong, active partnerships with each family will help you build a program that effectively and positively affects young children's experiences and learning.

Personal Identity

Culture influences who we are and who we become. Other influences on a person's identity include race, ethnicity, religion, education, gender, age, economic background, sexual orientation, and family structure. All of these things shape how we think about ourselves, how we make decisions or judgements, our overall approach to life, and how we respond to and interact with people that are different from us.

As a caregiver, you need to recognize and intentionally address your own personal identity, including your own biases and prejudices. Reflecting on our cultural backgrounds as well as our attitudes toward and interactions with those who are different from us is self-work that each of us as caregivers must do. All children require and deserve a caregiver who respects and values them, their family, and their culture. You should have an anti-bias approach in your program that is reflected and inherent in your attitudes and interactions with each infant and toddler and their families. For more information on anti-bias approaches and a list of resources, visit the National Association for the Education of Young Children (NAEYC) website, www.naeyc.org/anti-bias-education.

Cultural Approaches

People raise children using different approaches and ideas, including some strategies that are specific to individual regions and cultures. Although there is no one right way to do something, in licensed group care for infants and toddlers, programming and practices must adhere to health and safety guidelines set forth by state agencies. Accredited programs must also meet certain programming and teaching criteria set forth by a professional organization or group. It is helpful for you to be aware that some practices required by licensing agencies or encouraged by professional organizations may be different from what the families in your program typically do at home. To find out families' preferences, talk with them and ask about how they care for their infants and toddlers at home. Let families know that there are certain rules and guidelines that must be followed while children are in your care but that you will do your best to incorporate their cultural beliefs and preferences. The same is true when planning social-studies learning opportunities. By having this conversation, you are letting families know that you value their way of life and that you support their efforts to raise their children to be participating members of their home culture.

Approaches to Raising Children

Many different cultural ideas exist about how children should behave and what they need to know. Two common approaches to child rearing illustrate different ideas and attitudes as well as different intended results for children's behavior. One is the collectivist cultural approach, which emphasizes the interconnectedness of everyone in the family and cultural group. Families from collectivist cultures downplay independence and teach their children to be obedient, polite, and respectful of family members and the cultural group. Collectivist families want their children to learn to feel interdependent, and they use practices that promote children's reliance on and responsibility to others, including their family, extended family, and the whole cultural group. They want their children to be responsible for their behavior since what they do affects their family's standing within the cultural community. Belonging to a family and social group is very important to families in collectivist cultures.

The individualistic cultural approach is used by many families in the United States. This cultural perspective emphasizes being independent, self-reliant, and verbally expressive. Families who have an individualistic approach to child rearing may be concerned about their child's developing autonomy and uniqueness, which will set the child apart from everyone else. They focus on maximizing their child's individual success rather than on the child's interconnectedness to others.

Families have routines that are embedded in the schedules of their daily lives. These routines can include eating, sleeping, and toileting, as well as other aspects of family living. For example, mealtime routines include the way food is prepared, how and when it is served, who cleans up afterward, and how they do it. Families also have rituals that they perform daily or on special occasions, such as saying grace before a meal or before bedtime. Other rituals might include serving certain types of food on a specific day of the week or on holidays.

Families also have behavioral expectations for how children act and interact with others. A family's daily routines, rituals, and behavioral expectations are usually distinct and are learned from infancy. A family's approach to when and how to do certain things such as potty training, eating, sleeping, and daily schedules reflect a family's identity, values, and culture. Understanding and incorporating some of these rituals and routines into your program is an important aspect of social-studies learning for infants and toddlers, so it is critical to get to know each child and family and to think about how they differ from one another. This will allow you to create strong family partnerships that support the development and learning of each infant and toddler and will make activity planning easier.

Infant Sleeping Arrangements

Infant sleeping arrangements are traditional family practices that are usually passed from one generation to another. Today we know that putting infants on their backs to sleep and keeping pillows, blankets, bumper pads, stuffed toys, and other things out of the crib helps to prevent Sudden Unexpected Infant Death (SUID) and smothering. It is recommended that infants not sleep in an adult bed with other adults or children. When infants are able to roll over on their own, they may begin to choose to sleep on their stomachs or sides. However, a newborn and all young infants should be placed on their backs to sleep while they are in infant-toddler programs. Your licensing agency will have specific rules and guidelines for infant sleeping, which you should share with families. If you work in a state where licensing is not required, access safe infant sleeping information from organizations such as Zero to Three at www.zerotothree.org. The information found on the National Institute of Health website Safe to Sleep is another resource you can share with families. It can be found at www.nichd.nih.gov/sts/Pages/default.aspx.

Families who have an individualistic culture approach often have their children sleep in their own cribs that may also be in separate bedrooms. These babies sleep alone and not with someone else. When individualistic parents do have a baby sleeping in their bedroom, they often plan to move the baby to his own room a few months after birth. Individualistic parents want to see autonomy and individualism in their children. By contrast, families who have a collectivist approach may believe that an infant should not sleep in another room or even in a separate bed from her parents. Cosleeping is a common practice and a tradition that continues in many populations. Parents may feel that they can better respond to their infant's needs if the baby is kept close.

Talk with parents about the sleeping practices they are using at home with their infants. You should also provide information to families about safety and

SUID and let them know what type of sleeping arrangements will be used for their infant while in your care. Explain that you are required to follow certain rules about how infants are to sleep and that these methods are designed to help keep their infant safe. Since partnering with families is an important component of infant-toddler social studies, cultural sleeping practices and arrangements are important to know.

Eating

Eating and food are related to social-studies learning experiences, so it is helpful when planning activities to think about different cultural and family attitudes and approaches to feeding infants and toddlers. The family experiences that an infant or toddler has with food and eating will influence her likes and dislikes in food and her expectations about how food is prepared and presented. For example, families from collectivist cultures may breastfeed and spoon-feed their children longer than families who encourage more independence. Breastfeeding and spoon-feeding support the child's development of interdependence and cooperation. Breastfeeding in public may also be more acceptable. An extended duration of spoon-feeding children promotes patience and also models helpfulness to others since the child is being helped to eat. Individualistic families may encourage babies to begin to take part in feeding themselves as soon as possible. They may encourage their child to finger-feed or hold a spoon to try to get food to his mouth. Self-feeding promotes independence and self-help skills.

The types and quantities of food that families eat differ based on cultural heritage, preferences, and income. Talk with families about their approaches to breastfeeding and spoon-feeding, as well as the kinds of food eaten at home. You should include foods and practices in your program that are respectful to families' cultural heritages. This helps infants and toddlers feel comfortable and supported in their cultural identity, which leads to a positive sense of self.

It is never appropriate to use food for art or craft projects. In some cultures, food is scarce and revered. Some families may have experienced times when they did not have food or did not have enough food. It is also possible that they have survived food shortages or even famines. As you are planning learning experiences, you should also be aware of attitudes about wastefulness of food and attitudes regarding eating.

Schedules and Time

Cultural practices and beliefs about daily routines and schedules as well as when infants and toddlers are expected to perform certain tasks are components of social interactions and social studies. For example, some families think it is important to help an infant develop a consistent sleeping and eating schedule, and others think that infants should be fed when they are hungry and sleep when they are tired. The expectation that an infant should have a regular schedule of eating and sleeping reflects the belief that time needs to be structured and managed. Families who feel this way may not want to disrupt their infant's schedule.

Since licensing and/or accreditation guidelines require you to do certain things at certain times, a schedule and caregiving routines are very important in your program. Talk with families about group care and routines and how these are approached in your classroom. If possible, incorporate families' approaches and requests when you are able. There will be times when compromises will have to be made and other times when the health, safety, and well-being of each child and the group take precedence. Teachers may find that children whose families have different approaches to schedules may need time to adjust to the program's routines and schedules. In addition, many of the social-studies activities for infants and toddlers found in this book involve planning and conducting learning experiences around daily scheduled caregiving routines. Think about how you can help infants and toddlers form consistent eating, sleeping, and play schedules that are flexible but also predictable. Consistent and predictable caregiving routines help infants feel secure and provide opportunities for social-studies learning activities.

Potty Training

Social studies for infants and toddlers includes the development of a positive sense of self. During potty training, children learn self-help skills that support their growing need for independence and autonomy and help them to develop good feelings about their capabilities—which leads to a positive sense of self. You will want to understand families' approaches to potty training and then coordinate efforts between home and your program to support children's development of autonomy.

In collectivist cultures, families may start toilet training an infant when he is a few months old. The idea is that the child and caregiver develop signs that indicate it is time to use the toilet. Since infants are held most of the time, the caregiver learns the infant's behavior when he is getting ready to have a bowel movement, and then the caregiver immediately responds by holding the infant over a toilet. The caregiver may also train the infant by making a certain noise while the baby is being held over the toilet, which the child will then associate with toileting. The cooperation of the infant and caregiver is instrumental in this type of training, and children who have toileting accidents are not shamed. Potty training for families who have an individualistic approach is an important step in teaching a child to be independent. Many families in the United States begin teaching toileting when their child is around two years old or when the child shows interest. This individualistic approach gives the child the option of making her own choices. When this approach is used, toddlers must be aware that they are about to urinate or have a bowel movement, then communicate that need to the caregiver in time for the caregiver to help the child disrobe and sit on the potty. Several areas of development are involved in the child's ability to do this, including cognitive awareness of her body's signals for elimination; verbal ability to say she needs to go; physical muscle development to hold the urine and bowel movement for a period of time; and later, the motor skills to unbutton or unzip and pull down pants or underpants. This is a complicated process.

Diapering and toileting are topics to discuss with families when a child begins group care. It is a good idea for you to explain to families how diapering and toileting are approached in your program. Congruence of home practices and group-care practices may not always be possible, but respect for each family's approach is important. Children should never be made to feel bad or be shamed about toileting accidents or mistakes. Developing a positive sense of self and feeling independent and autonomous are basic components of infant-toddler social studies, and potty training provides an opportunity to help each child to develop these characteristics.

Child Behavior

Infant-toddler social studies includes children learning how to interact with and conduct themselves around others. Infants and toddlers begin to learn from their families how they are expected to behave at home and in public and how they are supposed to respond to and interact with other people. Just as families have different ideas about sleeping, eating, and toileting, they also have different expectations for their children's behavior and how to guide or discipline them. All social behaviors are learned, and the way that infants and toddlers are guided and disciplined influences their behavior and interactions with other people. Cultural differences influence the behavioral expectations families have for their child. In some family cultures, children are taught to be very respectful of adults, to not interrupt them when they are talking, to be quiet in the presence of adults, or perhaps not to speak directly to an adult authority figure. In some families, it is not acceptable for a child to act assertively and to be the center of attention. Children might be expected to defer to adults in one family, whereas in another family, the children interact with and talk to adults on an equal basis. Infants and toddlers begin to learn what social behaviors are expected within their family and with people outside of the family, as well as how they are supposed to act in public.

If you are not aware of family differences and the behavioral expectations families have for their children, you might misinterpret a child's behavior and the meaning behind it. For example, three-year-old Amy does not make eye contact or respond when a teacher asks her a question. Amy may have been taught that not making eye contact when speaking to an adult shows respect. I remember a parent who came to the guidance clinic where I worked as a child development specialist. The parent, Lucy, was concerned about her child because Shawn was having problems at school. His teacher, Georgia, said that she was concerned about Shawn's behavior and that he was not responding in class the way she thought he should. Georgia told Lucy that her son did not raise his hand or ask to be the first in line and that he did not want to be a "leader." It seemed that Georgia expected each child to be assertive, to raise his hand at every opportunity, and to want to be first in line. Georgia had an individualistic cultural orientation, and Shawn and Lucy had a collectivist cultural approach to social situations and interactions. Georgia's definition of a leader and the expectations she had for the children's behavior in her class reflected her culture. It is important for you as a caregiver to be respectful of differing approaches to raising children, to have realistic expectations for the children, and to give them opportunities to participate that are not shaped by one cultural expectation. These are imperative considerations since what you do and how you respond to children have long-lasting impacts. To establish realistic goals, take time to learn about the children's cultures and their families' approaches to child rearing. Also reflect on your own background and culture. You may discover that there is a need to make changes in your attitudes and the way you interact with and teach the children in your program.

To be an effective early childhood caregiver, you also need a solid understanding of social-emotional development and developmentally appropriate teaching and guidance strategies. Teaching and caring for infants and toddlers is different from the methods and approaches used for preschool and elementary-age children, and so are the discipline and guidance approaches. Since infants and toddlers thrive when they have healthy relationships, building a strong, positive relationship with each child is the foundation of infant-toddler guidance practices. Respecting the capabilities of each infant and toddler and having realistic expectations of what they all can and cannot do is another guidance strategy for this age group. When a toddler who is striving for autonomy says no to everything, it is a sign that he needs the opportunity to express his will and make choices. You can provide acceptable choices, such as "Would you like a piece of apple or banana?" If the child says no to both options, you should move on to avoid a power struggle. The child may even change his mind and make a choice at this point, because you allowed him time to feel some control over what he wants to eat.

Your knowledge of child development and the typical behaviors that infants and toddlers express will help you distinguish between typical development and behavior versus the need for assessment and potential intervention services for a child. You can refer young children with mental health issues, developmental delays, or other exceptional needs to agencies and services within your community.

A Developmental Approach to Social Studies for Infants and Toddlers

Families' culture, their own school experiences, and the learning goals they have for their children influence their expectations about what their children are taught and how. Social-studies learning goals and activities for infants and toddlers are different from those for older children. Because infant-toddler programming may be a new experience for families and their children, you can help them understand infant-toddler social studies and developmentally appropriate learning approaches.

Some families may expect to see infant and toddler caregivers using flash cards or workbooks, similar to the types of materials that are often used with older children, as tools for social-studies learning. However, the types of materials and teaching strategies used with preschool and elementary school children are not appropriate for babies and toddlers. As a caregiver, you can help by sharing with families and others in the community what developmentally appropriate programming for infants and toddlers is and why it is important. As defined in chapter 1, *developmentally appropriate* means using science-based knowledge about what babies can do, what they need, and how they grow, develop, and learn. Understanding developmentally appropriate practice and the child development theories and research that support this approach will help you explain why and how you do the things you do, including providing social-studies learning experiences for the infants and toddlers in your care.

Helping families and others understand why a developmentally appropriate approach is used with infants and toddlers is an important skill for caregivers. Families often ask early childhood caregivers questions about infant-toddler development and learning. When you provide families with developmental information and guidance, it helps them learn more about their children's development and shows them how to support their children's learning at home. It is important to respect the knowledge that families already have about their children and to ask them to share this knowledge with you. The sharing of information between families and caregivers is a vital component in infant-toddler programs and leads to the building of strong family-caregiver partnerships.

CHAPTER 3

Infant-Toddler Caregivers

As a caregiver, you have responsibility for society's young-est children, which includes offering them, through the care and teaching you provide, foundational experiences and interactions that will shape their future development, learning, capabilities, and successes. This is why attention to social-studies learning and infants' and toddlers' social-emotional development is so critical. By intentionally planning and providing social-studies learning opportunities in partnership with families, you will help build a solid base from which to launch young children onto a path of lifelong learning, healthy relationships, and social-emotional well-being.

Caregiving and Infant-Toddler Social Studies

The development of trust and emotional attachment during infancy lays a foundation for ongoing psychological well-being. When you provide dependable, responsive, and nurturing care, you are supporting an infant's positive sense of self and his social and emotional development. When a child receives warm and responsive care, he develops a positive mental model of relationships, which then influences how he feels about himself, how he responds to other people, and how he relates to and interacts with the environment. There are a few ways to go about this.

One type of care that is especially supportive of infant and toddler attachment assigns a primary caregiver to each child in the group. The primary caregiver is the one who changes the infant's diaper and feeds her while she is in group care. This strategy provides consistency for her and promotes feelings of security and attachment. Another strategy focuses on keeping groups of infants and toddlers together over time with the same teachers and same children. This also helps infants and toddlers to develop feelings of security and form emotional attachments to caregivers and other children. As the children become older and need different types of equipment and learning environments, the group moves to another room all together, along with their caregivers. This approach recognizes that infants and toddlers form attachments to one another just as they do to their siblings at home. These early attachments between young children form their first friendships and peer relationships. Social studies for infants and toddlers focuses on the development of a sense of self and learning how to interact with and relate to others and the environment. The strategies just described facilitate the development of these capabilities.

A more complete description of the NAEYC Standards, as well as its professional position statements on ethics, developmentally appropriate practices, and other topics related to early childhood education, are available online at www.naeyc.org.

Professional Standards and Ongoing Professional Development

The field of early care and education has identified specific knowledge, skills, and dispositions that define high-quality early childhood teaching. NAEYC has identified six broad standards and related key elements that are designed to guide you in your work with young children and families. The NAEYC Standards for Early Childhood Professional Preparation Programs identifies the types of knowledge and skills that teachers need. The following table shows the standards and elements.

NAEYC Standards for Early Childhood Professional Preparation

Standard 1: Promoting Child Development and Learning

Key Elements

- Knowing and understanding young children's characteristics and needs
- Knowing and understanding the multiple influences on development and learning
- Using developmental knowledge to create healthy, respectful, supportive, and challenging learning environments

Standard 2: Building Family and Community Relationships

Key Elements

- Knowing about and understanding diverse family and community characteristics

- Supporting and engaging families and communities through respectful, reciprocal relationships
- Involving families and communities in their children's development and learning

Standard 3: Observing, Documenting, and Assessing to Support Young Children and Families

Key Elements

- Understanding the goals, benefits, and uses of assessment
- Knowing about and using observation, documentation, and other appropriate assessment tools and approaches
- Understanding and practicing responsible assessment to promote positive outcomes for each child
- Knowing about assessment partnerships with families and with other professional colleagues

Standard 4: Using Developmentally Effective Approaches to Connect with Children and Families

Key Elements

- Understanding positive relationships and supportive interactions as the foundation of their work with children
- Knowing and understanding effective strategies and tools for early education
- Using a broad repertoire of developmentally appropriate teaching/ learning approaches
- Reflecting on their own practice to promote positive outcomes for each child

Standard 5: Using Content Knowledge to Build Meaningful Curriculum

Key Elements

- Understanding content knowledge and resources in academic disciplines
- Knowing and using the central concepts, inquiry tools, and structures of content areas or academic disciplines
- Using their own knowledge, appropriate early learning standards, and other resources to design, implement, and evaluate meaningful, challenging curricula for each child

Standard 6: Becoming a Professional

Key Elements

- Identifying and involving oneself with the early childhood field

(continued)

- Knowing about and upholding ethical standards and other professional guidelines
- Engaging in continuous, collaborative learning to inform practice
- Integrating knowledgeable, reflective, and critical perspectives on early education
- Engaging in informed advocacy for children and the profession

(NAEYC 2009)

As you begin to plan and teach the social-studies activities in this book, you should also pay attention to your own professional development and advancement of knowledge and skills. Attending to your own learning is essential. It will help you acquire more depth of knowledge and advanced caregiving skills and will boost your self-confidence, which will also help you to promote better outcomes for infants and toddlers.

The Infant-Toddler Caregiver Self-Assessments on the Web Components tab at www.redleafpress.org/itss are designed to help you assess your knowledge and skills, identify areas for growth, and plan your own professional development. The self-assessments include infant-toddler caregiving practices and skills that directly relate to providing effective infant-toddler social-studies learning experiences. You are the most important factor in the care and teaching of infants and toddlers, and as you acquire new knowledge and skills, you feel more confident and competent. Continually assessing yourself and advancing your knowledge and skills are powerful ways to affect the development and learning of infants and toddlers as well as to further your own professional growth.

Caregiver Attitudes, Beliefs, and Reactions

Just as infants and toddlers learn from their families, you, the caregiver, also learned from your family while you were growing up. We all learn attitudes and behaviors from our families and childhood environment that we often repeat as adults, especially those that are emotionally based. For example, you may have been required to eat all the food on your plate when you were a child. You may feel strongly about this and find yourself wanting infants and toddlers to not leave food on their plates. However, we now know that making children eat more than they want or need can lead to obesity and perhaps even ongoing issues about food. It is important for you to recognize that some of the behaviors and attitudes you learned while growing up may be different from the professional, scientifically researched care practices and techniques required in an infant-toddler classroom.

Child development theory and research findings support the use of positive constructive guidance and discipline strategies that help children develop self-control and self-discipline. The social-studies activities in this book address some of these practices. One example is teaching toddlers words to express their feelings; another is providing a place for toddlers to retreat to and be alone when they feel tired or overstimulated. Both strategies directly support a child's ability to develop social skills and self-discipline.

Self-awareness of your personal bias, attitude, hot spots, and blind spots is critical self-work that you must address in order to provide the best environment for the children in your care. A hot spot might be a personal aversion to certain behaviors. For example, a toddler who picks his nose may be a hot spot for you. If this "sets you off," then becoming aware of that is the first step. Then you must learn to modify your first reaction, which might be to say, "Stop that!" to "Let's find you a tissue to wipe your nose."

Blind spots may be more difficult for you to become aware of since they are aspects of ourselves that may be obvious to others but not to us. That is why they are called blind spots. Blind spots can be both positive and negative. For example, you may not be aware that you act differently toward one of the children in the group. You may be more impatient with this child than you are with the others. Perhaps the child reminds you of someone that you do not like. You may not be aware of these feelings and how they affect your caregiving and teaching of the child. Building self-awareness through self-reflection and specifically paying attention to attitudes and behaviors you might have that are noninclusive of those who are different from you is a first step in this situation. Next, it is important to work toward understanding how these attitudes affect the care and teaching of infants and toddlers in your program. This type of personal reflection will help you identify your hot spots and blind spots and become a more intentional caregiver. It also helps create a supportive social-studies learning environment for infants and toddlers.

Through self-reflection, you become intentional in what you do and how you do it. This is hard work, but over time, it pays off with new knowledge, attitudes, understandings, and skills that you can use to inform your partnerships with families and your interactions with the infants and toddlers in your care. The Infant-Toddler Caregiver Self-Assessments on the Web Components tab can help with this work.

Taking Time to Teach

Just as development and learning for infants and toddlers take time, so do planning and teaching. It is important to be intentional when choosing social-studies learning experiences for children. As a caregiver, you need to take time when you are planning activities to consider what the children are interested in learning and how they learn. Children's interests and what they want to learn are observable and often emerge through their behavior. Attentive observations are a powerful tool in developmental planning that lead to advances in children's learning. Observing the infants and toddlers in your care provides the basis for you to plan and scaffold experiences, be intentional in your interactions, and provide opportunities that build on children's prior knowledge.

A reflective teaching approach in infant-toddler classrooms helps children integrate new information and skills into their existing developmental framework and supports developmental advancement. Infants' and toddlers' understandings of self, other people, and how the world works are constantly evolving as you provide social-studies learning experiences and as the child's physical, social-emotional, communication, and cognitive capabilities develop. It is your job as the caregiver to observe, plan intentionally, and nurture each child's development.

Observing and Individualizing Learning Experiences

Infants and toddlers are competence motivated. That means that they want to be able to do things, to know how to use their bodies, to learn to talk, to learn about the world, and to be creative and solve problems. To capitalize on their drive for competence and provide the best social-studies learning opportunities, you must be intentional in your planning and teaching. Intentional teaching involves observing and watching a child to better understand his developmental capabilities and individual characteristics and needs. Reflecting on what you observe and asking questions such as, "What is the child trying to do?" or "What does the child's behavior mean?" are helpful in planning. Observations provide you with knowledge about how to adapt the environment and to plan supportive interactions and experiences that focus on children's needs and advance their learning and development.

Since each child is a unique individual with his own time frame for development, cultural and family expectations, and temperament characteristics, you need to observe and then plan and conduct learning experiences that support that child. You should objectively monitor and record each child's development on a regular basis. Checklists are available online for you to use during observations to document children's development and to guide your social-studies planning. For example, the Learning about Myself activity for eight- to twelve-month-old infants on page 68 would create an opportunity to observe an infant's growing self-awareness and reactions to seeing his image in the mirror. You could also observe to see whether he can point to his facial features and body parts.

Within the activity chapters in this book, summaries of the typical range of development for cognitive, language, social-emotional, and gross-motor and fine-motor development are included as a review of children's development. Use these developmental milestones summaries as you begin to plan and use the infant and toddler social-studies learning activities within that chapter. In appendix A, you will also find links to online developmental charts provided by early childhood professional organizations and agencies. The developmental checklists, the online development charts, and ongoing observations are all tools that will help you to best understand the infants and toddlers in your care and their capabilities at any given time.

You can also take short video clips of infants and toddlers as they play and interact with one another and the environment. These clips can help you identify children's current development and interests, which may help you complete developmental checklists. Use the reproducible observation forms in the appendixes (available at www.redleafpress.org/itss) to document infants' and toddlers' development and learning in response to the social-studies activities found in chapters 4 through 9. Repeat the activities over time and keep notes about how children's development and learning evolves. Teachers' observation of a child's different reactions and interactions over time provides evidence of the impact of the learning experiences on the child's development and learning.

You should create a portfolio for each child. The portfolio should include developmental observations, developmental checklists, temperament information, photographs, video clips, and individual child planning and learning plans and goals. Information from families about their children's development, culture, and other supportive materials can also be included in a child's portfolio. You can share the portfolios with families during conferences to show their children's development and how their learning is progressing.

Caregivers who want to work with infants and toddlers not only need to have close relationships with families, but they also need to establish strong emotional relationships with the young children in their care. The closeness of care required by infants and toddlers requires a certain kind of caregiver. Being comfortable with the type of physical care that infants and toddlers need and having a willingness to form an emotional bond are critical to supportive interactions that promote infant-toddler well-being. At the same time, there is ambiguity or uncertainty that what a caregiver is doing is actually promoting a child's development and well-being. This is because infants and toddlers do not talk or exhibit the types of learning behaviors that older children do.

Teaching through Interactions

The way you talk with infants and toddlers is a powerful teaching tool. You can purposefully use talking aloud to infants and toddlers to promote their language skills and communication, social-emotional development, and cognitive development. When planning for social-studies learning experiences, you can use the following ways of responding, describing, and talking aloud to infants and toddlers to achieve those goals:

1. Encouragement—Use encouragement to support infants and toddlers as they tackle new skills and try new things. Encouragement helps children develop confidence in their own abilities and promotes a positive, capable sense of self, because it focuses on and acknowledges a child's efforts and accomplishments. Praise is not the same as encouragement; praise is a judgment of quality, wrong or right, or bad or good. Praise trains a child to depend on adults' approval and constant feedback rather than teaching the child to do things for the natural enjoyment of exploration and learning. An example of encouragement is saying to an infant, "You are working hard to roll over. You can do it." When the infant does learn to roll over, you can say, "You did it," which puts the emphasis on the child's achievement and helps her to feel confident and good about herself. See appendix A on the Web Components tab for additional information, resources, and examples of encouragement.

2. Description—Explain aloud to an infant or toddler what is happening or what something looks like. For example, you might say, "The wind outside is blowing the leaves against the window." As caregivers, it is important for us to narrate and say aloud things that infants and toddlers need to hear so that they are able to learn about themselves, others, and the world around them.

3. Self-Description—Describe to infants and toddlers what you are doing. For example, you might say, "Now I am reaching for your clean diaper," as a child is being diapered. You can also describe how you are feeling. For example, "I feel tired and need a break."

4. Child-Description—Describe to infants and toddlers what they are doing or what you think they are feeling. For example, you might say to an infant, "You are kicking your feet," or to a toddler, "You picked up a piece of cookie and put it in your mouth" or "You feel happy and have a smile on your face."

5. Repeat and Expand Description—Restate aloud and expand on what a child has said or is trying to say. For example, you might respond to a toddler who says "baw" with "ball" or "You have a ball" or "You want to play with the ball" (whichever describes what you think the child is trying to say).

These ways of interacting are teaching strategies that you can use to expand children's learning. For example, look at the Sailing on the Ocean activity for two-year-olds on page 147. During this activity, you can use all these types of description to enrich the play and learning experiences of the toddlers. It may take some practice for you to learn and use these verbal teaching strategies, because as adults we have learned to think or talk to ourselves inside our heads. Practicing and using these talking strategies will result in powerful learning opportunities for infants and toddlers in your care.

Being in Tune with Infant and Toddler Cues

Being observant of infant and toddler behaviors and reactions will help you to know how to respond in ways that support their attempts to self-regulate. It will also help you to know when they are attentive and ready to learn or when they are tired and need a break. Infants and toddlers have so much to learn that it can become overwhelming for them. Through observation, you can learn what their behaviors mean. Since infants and toddlers cannot talk, they use body movements and other signals (cues) to let you know how they are feeling and what they need. Getting in tune with infant and toddler behaviors that signal their interest and attention and that they are ready to learn can guide teachers to know when to initiate social-studies learning activities. You can respond to an infant's cues by modifying your interactions and responses and by changing the environment. The emotional environment or tone of a classroom has to do with whether the atmosphere in the room is positive. Positive environments have a sense of comfort, happiness, and calmness. The physical environment is the way the room is arranged, the furniture, the noise level, the lighting, and the colors. Getting in tune with infants and toddlers means that you make modifications when needed to create more respectful and successful environments and learning experiences for young children.

Engaged and Ready to Learn

At birth, everything is new to an infant. Babies watch and try to make sense of what is going on around them. They are working hard to concentrate while dealing with new experiences. Infants want to learn, interact with the world, and be competent. They communicate how they are feeling, what they need, and what they are interested in seeing or doing through behavioral cues. A baby who wants to engage and interact may exhibit some of the following cues:

- An infant is relaxed.
- An infant watches you and what is going on around her.
- An infant makes noises that show his interest.
- An older infant may smile, kick his legs in excitement, or make happy sounds.
- An older infant or toddler smiles or makes eye contact.
- A mobile infant or toddler reaches for objects and people or moves toward what interests her.

Overstimulated, Afraid, Tired, or Needs a Rest

Babies are born with innate reflexes that are automatic responses to different events or stimuli. For example, infants are born with rooting and sucking reflexes that help them to find the nipple and eat. Another example is the Moro or startle reflex, which is a baby's response to suddenly being moved or to loud sounds. When startled, he throws back his head, extends his arms and legs, and then pulls his arms and legs in close to the body. Babies who startle may begin to cry and need to be picked up and comforted.

By about six months, infants begin to show fear of strangers. This is called *stranger anxiety*. Stranger anxiety increases from six months to nine months and continues to twelve months of age or longer. Crying and protest are common when infants are separated from their caregivers. As infants grow and develop, they watch what people do and begin to learn how they should react to things in their environments by the way adults react. They watch their caregiver's face and try to figure out the emotions of other people. This is called *social referencing,* and it is the way a baby uses the emotional cues of others to determine how to respond to strangers or to a particular situation. By the age of twelve months, a baby will look at her caregiver's face and know if the caregiver is afraid, angry, or happy. Children develop the ability to understand words (receptive language) before they can verbally say words (expressive language). So although infants and toddlers may not be able to verbally express themselves, they do begin to understand what is being said to and around them.

Infants get much better at reading adults' facial cues and expressions as they become toddlers. Since they learn about the world from those around them, young children may learn to fear the same things that their caregivers fear and to dislike or avoid the things their caregivers dislike and avoid. Understanding what infants and toddlers may fear or dislike given their experiences can help you reassure and comfort them in ways that help children feel more secure and trustful.

Since an infant can focus only on one or a few things at a time, a baby may become overstimulated if there is too much noise, too much to look at, or too many things happening. For example, playing music all day creates ongoing background noise that can be overstimulating for babies. The same is true when adults come on too strong, talking too much or too loudly. As infants are learning about the many things around them, they are also trying to learn to self-regulate and self-soothe. The development of these skills requires adult help. One way you can help is to recognize the behavioral cues that infants exhibit that may indicate overstimulation. Observe and respect a child's signals, and you will be able to stop or modify what is happening and address the child's needs. Below are some indicators that an infant or a toddler may be overstimulated, afraid, tired, hungry, or needing a break or rest:

- An infant closes her eyes or turns her face away.

- An infant frowns, or her face turns red.

- An infant begins to yawn, begins to cry, or becomes fussy.

- An infant turns his body away, arches his back, or squirms.

- An infant's or toddler's body, hands, or arms get stiff, or he may bring his hands to his face.

- An infant or toddler who is frightened may cry, cling to a caregiver, or hide his face.

- An infant or toddler who is hungry, tired, or frustrated may cry or have a tantrum.

Infants and Toddlers with Special Needs

As a caregiver, you are often the first person outside of a child's family to spend a significant amount of time with the child. If you are concerned that an infant may be experiencing difficulties or has a special need or disability, first talk with the child's family about your concerns. Remember that families feel responsible for their child and are sensitive to issues that involve a potential problem that their child may be experiencing. Build caring relationships with families and be thoughtful in the way you discuss their children with them. Put yourself in their place and think about how you would want someone to approach a serious topic regarding your child. Also, think about how you can connect families to community resources. Develop a resource file that includes brochures, flyers, and other information about community services for young children and their families. Design a bulletin board where families can access resource information. Have regular one-on-one meetings with families to discuss how their child is growing and developing. Provide information about agencies and programs in your community where an infant may be screened and assessed for potential services.

When you have a young child with defined special needs in your care, talk with the child's family, medical providers, occupational and physical therapists, or other interventionists for guidance on adaptations and approaches that ensure the child's inclusion in learning activities and the classroom.

Social-Studies Activities

Age-related developmentally appropriate activities and interactions designed to help infant-toddler teachers promote foundational social-studies learning and skills are presented in the remaining chapters. However, infants and toddlers should never be forced to do any of these activities. Interactions and learning opportunities should be pleasant experiences. If a child is tired, hungry, or emotionally upset or is experiencing difficulties of any type, the first priority of a teacher is to nurture, support, console, and attend to the baby's needs. Infants, toddlers, and young children who are forced to participate in learning activities may begin to avoid those types of experiences, which then creates additional issues.

CHAPTER 4

Social Studies for Infants Birth to 4 Months

During the first months of life, infants grow, develop, and change at a rapid rate. What happens during these early months and years has far-reaching influences on a child's future development and learning. It is during this time that babies begin to form emotional attachments to primary caregivers and to develop feelings of trust. Infants are born with reflexes that help them respond and adapt to their environments. These innate physical reactions are involuntary. They help infants survive. Babies do not control their reflexes. Rooting, sucking, startling, blinking, and grasping are reflexive at birth.

As infants grow, they begin to gain control of their bodies, beginning from the head down and from the center of the body outward. Motor development starts with the ability to control the head and center of the body first. By one month of age, babies begin to lift their heads, intently look at faces, follow movement with their eyes, respond to sounds, and make vocal noises. The reflexive smile of newborns becomes a social smile, especially when they hear their caregiver's voice or see their face.

By two months, infants hold their heads up for short periods of time, and their movements become smoother and more refined. They continue to watch and follow objects with their eyes. They gurgle and coo and smile in response to others, and they may laugh aloud. By the end of the second month, they may be able to lift their heads and shoulders up when placed on their tummies. Infants at three months hold their heads steady. They recognize faces, laugh, and smile. They also recognize voices and turn to loud noises and sounds. They make their own vocal sounds, such as squealing, cooing, and gurgling. By the end of the third month, some babies are rolling over, bringing their hands together, and beginning to reach for or bat at toys.

For the following activities, make a copy of the Infant-Toddler Social Studies Activity Observation (see appendix H on the Web Components tab at www

.redleafpress.org/itss) for each infant. Use the form to record how the infant responds to the activity. Describe how the infant's verbalizations, facial expressions, and body movements change as he develops. Remember that infants and toddlers with developmental delays, disabilities, or other special needs may need individualized adaptations for these activities. Adaptations should be designed and approved by a child's therapists. See page 30 for additional information.

Learning about Oneself

Temperament Characteristics

Area: Sense of Self

Developmental Objectives

- to learn about unique temperament characteristics
- to create a supportive caregiving environment
- to promote the development of a positive sense of self

Changing caregiver interactions and reactions and the environment in response to an infant's temperament style supports her ability to learn how to self-regulate, calm herself, and interact with others.

Instructions

- When an infant enters care, ask her family about her temperament traits and characteristics. Use this information to help her adjust to care by making adaptations that are responsive to the child's individual needs.
- When the child is in care, observe and take notes on her temperament traits and complete the IT3 temperament questionnaire (see appendix A online) for both the infant and yourself.
- After completing the questionnaires, use the suggested adaptations.

Extensions/Modifications

- Introduce new experiences and people more slowly for those infants who withdraw or become upset when new things are introduced in the environment.
- Help those infants who are irregular in their eating, sleeping, and elimination to be able to fit into the routines of the classroom and develop more regularity. Consistency in diapering, feeding, and playtimes helps infants learn routines. They begin to anticipate what is going to happen and when.
- Support infants who become upset more easily or whose intensity of emotions escalates quickly. Stay calm and begin to teach these infants how to calm and soothe themselves. For example, giving the infant a pacifier or holding and talking or singing to the infant may help.

Learning to Self-Regulate

Area: Sense of Self

Developmental Objectives

- to promote the abilities to self-regulate and calm self
- to promote the use of a comfort item

Instructions

- Ask the infant's primary caregiver what comfort items are used at home. Ask families to provide a duplicate of the comfort item for use while the infant is in care.
- Help the infant develop a way to self-regulate by consistently using the same item to help the child calm himself.

> Comfort items, such as a pacifier, are objects to help young infants calm themselves and begin to self-regulate. Another example is a cotton diaper or small receiving blanket covering the shoulder when a baby is burped. Over time, infants begin to associate the feel and smell of the cloth with the caregiver and may want to hold it while they sleep or need it to help calm themselves.

Extensions/Modifications

- Note that some comfort items are more useful and appropriate for infants than others. Infants will begin to hold on to a caregiver's hair, finger, or hand or hold the collar or sleeve of a caregiver's shirt. Be aware of what an infant is beginning to use as a way of comforting himself and then either support this or help him move toward a more suitable item. Holding the caregiver's hair while falling asleep may become problematic over time.

Calming Myself

Area: Sense of Self

Developmental Objectives

- to promote the abilities to self-regulate and calm self
- to promote the ability to fall asleep on her own

Instructions

- Quickly respond to babies; comfort and soothe them when they are upset and need your help to calm down.
- To calm a crying infant, gently rub or pat her back as you hold her.
- Talk in a soothing voice or be silent if the child is overstimulated.

- Walk around the room, sit on the floor, or rock in a chair with the infant in your arms.
- Allow infants to move their hands to their mouths to suck on, or let them use a pacifier if the child's family approves.

Extensions/Modifications

- Give each family back-to-sleep information regarding the safety of infant sleeping procedures and a copy of child care licensing requirements for infant sleeping procedures and guidelines. See page 13 for information on SUID and sleeping.
- Ask the family what routine is used when putting the infant down to sleep, and then use this same routine to help her adjust.
- Sleeping arrangements for infants vary from culture to culture. You can be respectful of

- Put infants on their backs to sleep before they completely fall asleep in your arms. This helps an infant to learn to calm and soothe herself and to fall asleep on her own.

differences in sleeping arrangements while at the same time adhering to safety and licensing rules while infants are in your care. An infant who has been cosleeping with a family member or who has been sleeping on her stomach may have difficulty sleeping in care. Be patient and supportive with infants who are learning new sleeping positions as well as getting used to a new sleeping environment. Sing songs or sit near and pat the baby.

Looking at My Image in a Mirror

Area: Sense of Self

Developmental Objectives

- to help an infant look at himself in a mirror
- to promote the development of a positive sense of self

Instructions

- Allow enough time for the infant to feel comfortable in the environment and with the people who are present before initiating this activity.
- Hang an unbreakable mirror on the wall of the classroom. Keep a handheld unbreakable mirror in the classroom as well.

- Hold the infant so that he can see his image in the mirror.
- Call him by name and talk to him about his image.
- Encourage the infant to look at your image as well as his and to make eye contact in the mirror.

Extensions/Modifications

- With the infant on your lap, hold an unbreakable handheld mirror so he can see his

image. Call him by name and talk with him about his image.

Infant Cues

Area: Sense of Self

Developmental Objectives

- to recognize, respect, and respond to each infant's cues
- to promote the development of a positive sense of self

> Being attentive to cues and then respecting what children are trying to communicate helps infants feel good about themselves and their abilities to interact with others.

Instructions

- Learn about each infant's unique temperament traits and personality and then respond respectfully, helping the baby feel comfortable with her environment and the people in it.
- When feeding babies, be attentive to satiation cues. When you think a baby is full, verbally ask, "Are you full?" and stop feeding her.
- Be attentive to cues that indicate that a child might be overstimulated, tired, too hot, or too cold, or in need of attention.
- See chapter 3 for a listing of infant behaviors that indicate overstimulation.

Extensions/Modifications

- Help families learn about infant eating cues, food, and nutrition.
- Talk with families about how their infant communicates when she is hungry and when she is full. Invite an infant nutritionist to give a workshop for families.
- Develop a bulletin board display that features information on infant nutrition and suggestions for helping infants and toddlers develop good attitudes about food, healthy eating habits, and exercise.

Respecting Infants as People

Area: Sense of Self

Developmental Objectives

- to promote feelings of respect and value
- to promote the development of a positive sense of self

> During the first months, infants exhibit several reflexes, including the Moro or startle reflex, which usually disappears by four months. Picking up, dressing, and diapering newborn babies will often startle them. Some have a more exaggerated startle reflex.

Instructions

- Make eye contact and tell the infant what you are going to do before you do it. For example, "I am going to pick you up and change your diaper."

- Take time to use each caregiving routine as an opportunity for the baby to begin to form positive feelings about himself and learn about his body by talking to him.

Extensions/Modifications

- When changing a baby's diaper, tell him whether he is wet or has had a bowel movement. Avoid making faces or negative comments about his elimination and bodily processes.
- Talk with families about teaching their baby accurate names for genitalia but follow their

- While dressing, diapering, and holding the baby, verbally name his legs, arms, toes, fingers, feet, head, and other body parts.

wishes. This can be a sensitive topic, and families may have varying cultural approaches and attitudes.
- Be sensitive to the infant's startle reflex and make slow, deliberate movements to reduce this reaction and to help him remain calm and self-regulate.

Developing Attachment to a Caregiver

Area: Sense of Self

Developmental Objectives

- to provide continuity of care
- to promote attachment to a caregiver
- to promote the development of a positive sense of self

Instructions

- Assign each infant a primary caregiver who establishes consistent caregiving routines that are based on the infant's needs, including feeding, changing, picking up, holding, cuddling, talking, and singing.
- Provide predictable care so the infant learns that her needs will be recognized and met

and she feels secure and able to regulate her emotions.
- Respond to the infant's needs before she becomes inconsolable.
- Verbally label what you think the child is feeling and respond with the type of care needed.

Extensions/Modifications

- Infants' temperament characteristics and traits may affect how quickly they calm down and what types of soothing strategies

work best. Learn about each child's unique temperament characteristics and adjust your interactions to support her needs.

Recognizing and Responding to Infants' Needs

Area: Sense of Self

Developmental Objectives

- to recognize and respond to communication attempts and needs
- to promote the development of self-regulation and delay of gratification

Instructions

- Talk to an infant from across the room to communicate that you are near when you cannot immediately respond to him.
- Use the tone and different pitches of your voice to communicate that you are aware that the infant is communicating with you about how he is feeling.
- Verbally let an infant know that you will help him as soon as you can.
- When you do respond to an infant, say, "Thank you for waiting." Then say, "You are hungry and needed my help" or "You were tired of being alone and needed me to pick you up," just as you would say to an adult who has been waiting for you or who needed your attention.
- Respect the infant as a person and use words such as, "I'm sorry" or "thank you."
- Acknowledge his needs and feelings and model words that you want him to learn.

> Infant classrooms are busy places, and teachers cannot always immediately respond to an infant's needs. However, you can communicate to infants that you know they need you and that you are coming as soon as you can.

Extensions/Modifications

- Sing a soothing song or make up a song to sing that responds to what you think the infant needs. For example, sing, "I am coming, I am coming, yes I am, yes I am" to the tune of "Twinkle, Twinkle, Little Star."

Learning to Relate to and Interact with Other People

My Family Caregivers

Area: Family

Developmental Objectives

- to promote attachment to home caregivers
- to promote the development of a positive sense of self

Instructions

- Take photographs of the faces of the infant's home caregivers.
- Print the photographs and laminate them or place them in a plastic sleeve.
- Throughout the day, hold the infant and show her her family caregivers' photographs.
- Talk with her about her family members, calling her primary caregivers by name in their home language.
- Point to the caregivers' eyes, noses, mouths, and hair as you talk with the infant about her caregivers.
- Repeat this activity or the following modification daily.

Extension/Modification

- Put the photographs of the infant's caregivers on the wall or on a display board at the infant's eye level. Talk to her about the photographs and call the caregivers by name.

Families and Culture

Area: Family

Developmental Objectives

- to learn about family and culture
- to create a multicultural classroom environment representative of all families
- to promote a sense of belonging to a family and culture

Instructions

- Ask the infant's family members what language is spoken at home, what foods are eaten, what some family rituals are, and about how they care for their child.

- Learn some basic words in the infant's home language. Use these words during interactions and caregiving routines with him.

Extensions/Modifications

- Get to know his family members.
- Talk with him about his family and call them by name.
- Use items from the family's culture in the classroom to create a more familiar environment for him.
- Play music from his family's culture.

Infant Crying as Communication

Area: Communication

Developmental Objectives

- to recognize and respond to communication attempts
- to promote language and communication development

> Notice that infants change the way they cry, depending on their needs. These cries vary based on how they are feeling either emotionally or physically.

Instructions

- Respond to the infant when she cries and say aloud what it is you think she is feeling or needing.
- Use words or short phrases such as "You are hungry" or "You need me to hold you." This helps her first attempts at communication be successful.

Extensions/Modifications

- Notice when the infant turns her head toward you (or someone) while you are talking. Say, "You hear me talking" and then talk directly to her using the different types of communication discussed on pages 26–27.

Making Sounds and Learning How to Communicate

Area: Communication

Developmental Objectives

- to recognize and respond to communication attempts
- to promote language and communication development

Instructions

- When an infant makes sounds, such as vowel sounds like *ah* or *uh*, respond to him by repeating the same sounds.
- Take turns "talking" with him, waiting for him to make a sound and then imitating the same sound. Also, respond with words when he yawns, stretches, or makes other sounds or body movements.

Extensions/Modifications

- Model language by verbally describing what you are doing during caregiving routines and as he watches you and other babies.
- Use words to describe his facial expressions and what he may be feeling.

Hearing Songs and Lullabies

Area: Communication

Developmental Objectives

- to promote language development
- to promote awareness of music and songs

Instructions

- Sing songs and lullabies to the infant while holding her in your arms. Hold her so she can see your face.
- Learn songs and lullabies in her home language and sing them to her.

Extensions/Modifications

- Sway to the music and sing along.
- Encourage the infant to "sing" with you.

Looking at Books

Area: Communication

Developmental Objectives

- to promote language development
- to promote early literacy skills

Instructions

- Begin to show and read simple board books to the infant.
- Show him books with one picture on a page.
- Hold him on your lap as you read.

- Point to the picture on each page with your finger and name the picture.

Extensions/Modifications

- Read simple books that have rhymes and repetition of phrases.
- Hold the infant on your lap and read or play tapes of simple books in his home language.
- If you speak the home language, read along with the tape.
- Point at pictures in a book and talk with the infant about them.

Looking at Other Babies

Area: Social Skills

Developmental Objectives

- to promote social skills and social development
- to promote awareness of other infants

Instructions

- Hold an infant in your arms so she can see another baby.
- Call the other baby by name and talk to the infant in your arms about the other child.
- Introduce the infants to each other, calling each by name.
- Describe the other child to the infant you are holding.
- When the infants make eye contact, talk with them about looking at each other.
- Repeat their names often.

Extensions/Modifications

- Be sensitive to each infant's reactions, cues, and facial expressions. Describe these to the infants.
- Say aloud what you think each infant is feeling.

Touch

Area: Social Skills

Developmental Objectives

- to learn how to touch another infant
- to promote social skills and social development

Instructions

- As the infant gets older and begins to reach, model for him how to gently touch someone else.
- Place two babies close enough so they can reach out and touch each other.
- Sit close and talk to each baby.
- Describe how the infants react and what their feelings may be when they are being touched or when they are touching the other baby.
- Watch each infant's facial expressions.
- Listen for vocalizations and model conversation turn-taking when talking to the babies.

Extensions/Modifications

- Each day, change the pairings so that each child has this experience with every other child in the room.

Playtime

Area: Social Skills

Developmental Objectives

- to learn to play near another infant
- to promote social skills and social development

Instructions

- During tummy floor time, place two infants a few feet apart and facing each other.
- Put a toy on the floor between them.
- Lie down with them or sit close.
- Encourage each child to lift her head up to see the toy.
- Talk about the toy and what each infant is seeing, including the other baby.
- Call each child by name and give each verbal encouragement as both develop the ability to raise their heads and look at toys and each other.

Extensions/Modifications

- Each day, change the pairings so that each child has this experience with every other child in the room.

Learning to Relate to and Interact with the Environment

Looking at Toys in the Classroom

Area: Classroom Community

Developmental Objectives

- to promote development and learning within the classroom community
- to promote awareness and exploration

Instructions

- Place the infant on her tummy in a safe area and put a small stuffed animal or toy to the side where she can see it.
- After a few minutes, move the toy to the other side of the infant.
- Next, put it in front of the infant.
- Talk with the baby about the toy and encourage her to raise her head and look at it.

Extensions/Modifications

- Change her location in the room so she experiences a different view of things.
- Describe to and talk with her about what she sees.
- Use different types of toys and objects that vary in size and color for the infant to look at and try to reach for.
- Move objects closer or farther away to change the way they look to her.

Lying on the Floor and Looking at Another Infant in a Mirror

Area: Classroom Community

Developmental Objectives

- to develop connectedness to others within the classroom community
- to promote a sense of belonging to a classroom community

Instructions

- Securely attach an unbreakable mirror to the wall at floor level.
- During floor time, place two infants side by

side on their tummies a few feet from the mirror.

- Sit or lie down close to the children.

- As the infants raise their heads, encourage them to look in the mirror at the reflections.
- Call yourself and each child by name as you talk about the images in the mirror.

Extensions/Modifications

- Each day, change the pairings so that each child has this experience with every other child in the room.

Looking at Other Infants' Pictures

Area: Classroom Community

Developmental Objectives

- to promote awareness of other infants in the classroom
- to promote a sense of belonging to a classroom community

Instructions

- Take a photograph of each infant and make a class photo album.
- While holding an infant on your lap, look at the photograph album.

- Call all children by name and describe them, pointing to eyes, nose, mouth, and ears.

Extensions/Modifications

- Help the infant be aware of other infants in the classroom by having arrival and departure rituals. For example, when you or the child's family member brings the infant into the room where the other infants are, say, "Let's all say good morning to Eva," or when she leaves at the end of the day, say to the

group, "Eva is going home. Good-bye, Eva. See you tomorrow."

Playing with and Batting Toys Near Another Infant

Area: Classroom Community

Developmental Objectives

- to interact with different types of toys within the classroom community
- to play near another infant

Instructions

- As an infant's motor skills develop, put bars with hanging toys near for him to reach out and bat.
- Place two or more infants side by side on their backs each with his own bar of hanging toys.

- Describe what each infant is doing to the other infant, calling each by name.
- Show joy and excitement in the discoveries made by each child and encourage exploration.

Extensions/Modifications

- Change the pairings daily so infants get to play near everyone in the classroom.

Looking at Art

Area: Broader Community and Society

Developmental Objectives

- to promote awareness of and interaction with the environment
- to promote a connection to the broader community

Instructions

- Collect posters of artwork displayed in local museums or from museums around the world. Laminate and display the posters at the children's eye level in the classroom.

- Hold the infant close to a poster and talk with her about what she is seeing. Talk about colors, textures, shapes, and objects in the art.

Extensions/Modifications

- Regularly change and display posters of different types of art, including paintings, sculptures, baskets, and pottery.

Talking a Walk around the Inside of the Building

Area: Broader Community and Society

Developmental Objectives

- to provide experiences and interactions with the larger environment
- to promote language development

Instructions

- Hold an infant in your arms or place him in a stroller.
- Walk outside the classroom (but inside of the building) to show the infant different things.
- As you walk, talk with the infant about what he is seeing. See pages 26–27 for different types of descriptions you can use with infants.
- If you see other people on your walk, call them by name and describe what they are doing.

Extensions/Modifications

- Be attentive to signs of overstimulation and be respectful of his needs for fewer rather than more things and people to look at.

Going for a Neighborhood Walk

Area: Broader Community and Society

Developmental Objectives

- to provide experiences with the larger community
- to promote awareness of and connection to the larger community

Instructions

- Put an infant in a stroller and take her outside for walks around the building—and neighborhood, if safety permits.
- Stop often, kneel beside the stroller, and talk to the infant about what she is seeing.
- Talk about how the air feels on her face and skin, what she is smelling, the colors she is seeing, and the sounds she is hearing.

Extensions/Modifications

- Since the outside environment changes with the seasons, take the infant outside in a stroller often so she can experience the different seasons and changes in the neighborhood.

CHAPTER 5

Social Studies for Infants 4 to 8 Months

• •

By four months, most babies have begun to settle into in-creasingly consistent routines of eating, sleeping, and activity. From four to eight months of age, children begin to gain more control of their bodies and movements and begin to more actively explore the environment through the use of their increasing motor skills. They smile socially at others and express their feelings through facial expressions and emotional reactions. They show strong attachments to specific adults and begin to distinguish people they know and trust from people they do not know. Parents and caregivers learn more about infants' individual characteristics as they gain in developmental capabilities. The same type of ongoing, consistent caregiving described in the previous chapter continues to be important.

By four months, infants respond with coos and other sounds when someone talks to them. They hold their heads steadier and can raise their heads and chests up off the floor or bed when placed on their tummies. They reach for objects and can grasp a toy in their hands. Infants five months of age can usually roll over and may be able to sit for a few seconds. They notice bright, bold colors and reach for objects, often placing them in their mouths. They babble and notice new sounds and will turn their head toward the sounds to listen attentively. They may begin to notice strangers and become anxious around new people.

Infants can roll from stomach to back and back to stomach usually by six months. At this age, they begin to sit by themselves without support. When on their tummies, they may lunge forward and may even start to crawl. Some babies roll where they want to go and use these movements to begin to explore the broader physical environment. Seven-month-old infants continue reaching for things and picking up objects, and they like to bang things together. They may pick up something in one hand and then pass it to their other hand. They begin to make simple gestures, such as waving bye-bye. By eight months, they may be able to stand, supporting their weight on their legs while holding onto something.

For the following activities, make a copy of the Infant-Toddler Social Studies Activity Observation (see appendix H on the Web Components tab at www .redleafpress.org/itss) for each infant. Use the form to record how the infant responds to the activity. Describe how the infant's verbalizations, facial expressions, and body movements change as he develops. Remember that infants and toddlers with developmental delays, disabilities, or other special needs may need individualized adaptations for these activities. Adaptations should be designed and approved by a child's therapists. See page 30 for additional information.

Learning about Oneself

Routines

Area: Sense of Self

Developmental Objectives

- to promote the development of a positive sense of self
- to promote the ability to self-regulate

> Rituals help infants to understand what is about to happen and helps them to begin to self-regulate.

Instructions

- Create rituals and routines for when an infant arrives and when he leaves. For example, sing or say a greeting or a good-bye song.

- Establish routines and rituals to use throughout the day. For example, play a quiet lullaby as you help infants get ready to nap as a signal to them that it is time to go to sleep.

Extensions/Modifications

- Learn words related to routines in the infant's home language and say or sing in both English and his home language.

> When infants hear languages other than English in the classroom, they are experiencing cultural diversity.

Respecting Me as a Person

Area: Sense of Self

Developmental Objectives

- to promote the development of a positive sense of self
- to recognize and care for each infant as an individual

Instructions

- Respect the infant as a person by telling her what you are going to do next. For example, tell her that you are going to pick her up and that it is time to get her diaper changed. Engage the child in what is happening in the classroom and encourage her help and cooperation.

- During diapering, talk to the infant and describe what you are doing. Rather than distracting a child with a toy, engage the child in a "conversation."
- Be aware of your facial expressions and tone of voice as you interact with infants.

Extensions/Modifications

- As the infant gets older and begins to roll over and become more active, engage her

cooperation during caregiving routines and learning activities in the classroom.

Learning about Myself

Area: Sense of Self

Developmental Objectives

- to promote the development of self-awareness
- to promote the development of a positive sense of self

Instructions

- Hold an infant on your lap as you sit on the floor or in a chair in front of a mirror that has been securely hung on the wall.
- Talk to him about his image in the mirror. Point to his body parts and name them.
- Describe the infant to him. For example, "You have curly hair."

- Call the child by name as you describe his characteristics.
- Use different types of description to talk with the infant as you look in the mirror. See pages 26–27 to review types of talk with infants.

Extensions/Modifications

- Sit on the floor with two infants on your lap in front of a mirror.

- Describe both children, using their names.

Building Trust and Calming Myself

Area: Sense of Self

Developmental Objectives

- to promote the development of trust
- to promote the ability to self-regulate

Instructions

- When an infant needs attention, speak aloud to her and reassure her that you are nearby and will be coming.
- Continue to talk to her as you get ready to assist her. Make eye contact if possible and call the baby by name.
- Verbally label what you think the baby needs or feels.

Extensions/Modifications

- Learn each infant's temperament style and adapt the above strategies to meet the individual needs of each child. Complete the temperament questionnaire from the Center for Infant Mental Health at www

Caregivers may not always be able to immediately respond to an infant. When you're engaged in an activity across the room or a few feet away from an infant, continually observe for facial expressions, changes in facial color, verbalizations, and body movements that indicate that the child is in need of attention.

- Try to go to the infant before she begins to cry and gets upset and/or out of control.

.ecmhc.org/temperament/ for each infant on a regular basis to review and inform your interactions, needed adaptations, and changes in yourself or the infant.

Getting Frustrated

Area: Sense of Self

Developmental Objectives

- to promote the development of motor skills
- to promote the development of persistence
- to promote the ability to self-regulate

Instructions

- Stay near as the infant begins to learn to sit alone, roll over, and pull up. Watch for signs

As infants learn new motor skills, they may become frustrated or upset when trying to move or do something new with their bodies. Learning how to cope with frustration is a component of self-regulation.

of frustration and verbally describe the child's behaviors and feelings.

- Encourage his attempt to learn to move and control his body. For example, you could say, "You are trying very hard to roll over. You can do it."
- Describe what you think he is trying to do.

Extensions/Modifications

- Use different types of description to help the infant learn words for his feelings and behaviors. See pages 26–27 for a description of types of talk to use with infants and toddlers to promote development and learning.

- Do not immediately intervene unless health or safety is an issue. Give the infant an opportunity to try to solve the problem.
- Encourage infants who are reluctant or who become frustrated easily to try new things and not give up.

Waking Up

Area: Sense of Self

Developmental Objectives

- to recognize and support individual characteristics
- to promote the development of a positive sense of self

Instructions

- When an infant wakes up, greet her softly and with a smile. Say, "I see you are awake." Hold your arms out and say, "I'm going to pick you up now." Pick up the baby and hold her close.
- Do not rush the baby to an immediate diaper change after she wakes. Give the child time to wake up and transition back into the room.

- For an infant who wakes up more slowly, pick her up and allow her to lay her head on your shoulder as you carry her into the play area.
- Sit down in a chair or on the floor with the child on your lap. As the child wakes up, you can ask, "Are you awake and ready to change your diaper?"

Extensions/Modifications

- Adapt your approaches and interactions based on each infant's individual characteristics. Some infants may be ready to transition more quickly from sleep to a diaper change and then rejoin the classroom after a nap.

Area: Sense of Self

Developmental Objectives

- to recognize and support individual needs
- to promote the development of a positive sense of self

Instructions

- Provide a variety of tactile experiences with different types of textures while observing the infant's reactions.
- Make adjustments and adaptations to allow for exploration while at the same time being sensitive to those textures that are not pleasant for him to experience.

Some infants are more sensitive than others to textures, including the textures of clothing, toys, upholstery, floorings, and food. As infants begin to rake and grasp objects and to bring them to their mouths, you can observe for differences in how infants experience texture. Some infants may react in a defensive way to the feel of certain textures.

Extensions/Modifications

- Some objects, toys, fabrics, or other materials have odors that may be off-putting, or even harmful, to infants. For example, some plastic toys and dishes have strong odors and additives that are harmful, especially if mouthed by infants. Check manufacturing labels and choose toys and other items that are safe for infants.
- Do not wear perfumes or put potpourri in the classroom. Some adult hair products also have strong scents, and infants may be sensitive or even allergic to these. Check with families regarding infants' allergies and sensitivities to textures, odors, and other substances.
- If you smoke tobacco products, you should not wear clothing in the classroom that has been exposed to tobacco smoke while caring for infants or toddlers.

Learning to Relate to and Interact with Other People

My Family

Area: Family

Developmental Objectives

- to promote the development of attachment
- to promote partnerships with families

Instructions

- Ask the family to bring a group photograph that includes every family member who lives in the infant's home.
- Ask who each person is and what the infant is being taught to call each person.
- Create a photograph album or photograph display that you can look at with the infants.

- Hold an infant on your lap and look at his family's photograph. Point to the family members, call them by name, and describe them. For example, say, "This is your grandpa. He has on a brown hat." Make sure to use the names that the infant is learning to call these people in his home.

Extensions/Modifications

- As the infant begins to sit alone and hold things in his hands, make a copy of his family's photograph on card stock or laminate it onto a piece of thin cardboard.
- Let the infant hold and look at his family's photograph. Sit close and talk with him about his family, calling each person by name.
- Take a photograph of the infant and put it on the opposite side of the cardboard so he has a photo of himself to look at along with his family.

My Family's Music

Area: Family

Developmental Objectives

- to promote awareness and enjoyment of music
- to promote connections to family culture

Instructions

- Collect music that is representative of the infant's family and culture.
- Hold the infant on your lap as you play music. Sing along and encourage her to sing along with you. Watch her facial expressions and reactions.
- Verbally describe the child's reactions to her. For example, if the child begins to bounce or move to the music say, "You are moving to the music."
- Hold an infant while you stand and move and sway to the music with her.
- Do not have music playing in the background all day. Play music and songs when you are available to interact with an infant or small group of infants.

Extensions/Modifications

- Ask each family to make recordings of songs they sing, instruments they play, or rhymes they say to their child at home. If a family speaks a language other than English, ask that the song be in their home language.
- As the infant begins to vocalize to the music, record her singing and share these recordings with her family.

My Family Rituals

Area: Family

Developmental Objectives

- to promote family culture and rituals
- to promote partnerships with families

Instructions

- Encourage families to have drop-off and pickup routines or rituals. This will help both babies and families during transition into and out of the program each day.

Extensions/Modifications

- Observe the way that a family displays emotions and other cultural behaviors. Be sensitive to these differences and think about how infants learn these and display them while in care. Be alert to your own personal or cultural biases regarding behavioral differences and be careful not to judge infants and families based on these biases.

Each family may have a specific way to show affection, to say good-bye in the morning, and to reunite at the end of the day. Observe and help each family to develop a ritual for these times. It may be helpful, for example, if an infant has something to hold as she goes from her family member's arms to the teacher's. Some families like to hug and kiss one another, whereas others are more reserved in the way they show affection.

Making Sounds to Imitate

Area: Communication

Developmental Objectives

- to promote verbalization
- to promote the concept of taking turns
- to promote language and communication development

Instructions

- Hold an infant on your lap and make sounds for her to imitate. Wait for her to respond, and then repeat the sound.
- Also imitate the sounds she makes. Wait for her to respond, and then repeat.
- Make different movements with your mouth such as puckering your lips, clicking your tongue, and whistling. Pause afterward and wait for the infant to respond.

Extensions/Modifications

- Learn and use sign language for frequent caregiving activities (eat, change, sleep), familiar objects, and feelings. Look for opportunities to use these signs, while at the same time saying the word.

Hearing Words and the Names of Objects, People, and Feelings

Area: Communication

Developmental Objectives

- to promote language development
- to promote visual recognition of emotions
- to learn words for emotions

Instructions

- Collect photographs of people doing various jobs and activities, such as reading, cooking, cleaning, dancing, eating, playing sports, or playing with toys. Show infants the photographs and talk with them about what the people are doing and the objects they are using.
- Show infants photographs of people's faces showing different emotions. Say aloud what each person is feeling to help infants learn words for emotions.
- Learn a few words describing emotions in an infant's home language and use them to describe the people in the photographs.

Extensions/Modifications

- Make different types of faces to show emotion for infants to imitate and say, "This is my happy face" or "This is my sad face."

Looking at Books

Area: Communication

Developmental Objectives

- to promote language and communication development
- to provide experiences enjoying books, looking at pictures, and hearing someone read

Instructions

- Look at and read simple books to an infant while you hold him on your lap.
- Use books with one or two pictures on a page. Point to the pictures as you read the book.
- Read the same books over and over again so that the infant becomes familiar with the pictures, words, and story.

Extensions/Modifications

- Encourage the infant to point at the pictures or to hold your finger as you point at the pictures. Give him time to look at the pictures before turning the page.
- Respond to his facial expressions and movements as you read.
- Elaborate on his body movements and attempts at vocalizations. When he babbles or bounces excitedly as you read and look at pictures in a book, respond with a word or short sentence that relates to what he is seeing. For example, say, "Puppy. You see the puppy."

Helping a Friend

Area: Social Skills

Developmental Objectives

- to promote the development of empathy
- to promote the development of prosocial interactions

At birth, an infant will cry when he hears another infant crying. In care, infants may get upset and begin to cry in response to another infant's distress and crying.

Instructions

- Reassure an infant who cries in response to another infant's distress.
- Let him know that the other infant is being cared for and will be all right.
- Verbally label what each infant is feeling. For example, say, "John, you hear Sybil crying. She is hungry and is going to get her bottle soon" or "John, are you upset because you hear Sybil crying? She is going to be okay."
- Call both infants by name.

Extensions/Modifications

- As the infant becomes more mobile, he will sometimes try to comfort another infant that is in distress. These are signs of empathy. Model how to gently pat or hug another infant.
- Verbally say aloud what each child is feeling and doing. When one infant is trying to comfort another, say, "You are trying to help Mike feel better. You like Mike and want to help."

Sitting Together

Area: Social Skills

Developmental Objectives

- to promote the development of social awareness
- to promote the development of early friendships

Instructions

- Roll up a blanket into a tube and form it into a circle on the floor. Sit two infants in the circle facing each other, with the blanket supporting who cannot sit alone.
- Sit near the children and talk with them about each other.
- Call them both by name and encourage them to touch their feet together or to reach out with their hands and touch the other's feet.
- Change the pairings of children so that each infant has this experience with every other child in the room.

Extensions/Modifications

- When two infants are able to sit alone, sit them on the floor and put a toy between them. Sit close and encourage each child to reach out and bat or touch the toy. Call them both by name and describe what they are doing.

Looking at a Book with a Friend

Area: Social Skills

Developmental Objectives

- to promote the development of social awareness
- to promote the development of early friendships

Instructions

- Sit on the floor with two infants on your lap. Look at a board book together.
- Call each child by name and encourage the children to gently touch and interact with each other as the three of you look at pictures in the book.
- Change the pairings of children so every infant has this experience with every other child in the room.

Extensions/Modifications

- As infants learn to sit alone, encourage them to look at books or play with toys near one another. Sit close and call each child by name.
- Model how to reach, pick up toys, shake, or bang toys.
- Model how to be near another person, how to look at books, and how to play.

Practicing Motor Skills Near Another Infant

Area: Social Skills

Developmental Objectives

- to practice motor skills in a safe play space
- to provide an opportunity for infants to be close to one another in the classroom
- to promote the development of social awareness

Instructions

- Provide space on the floor for two infants to sit, roll, and crawl.
- Place two infants near each other in the play space. Sit near and support infants who are learning to sit alone, roll over, and crawl.
- Call both children by name and describe what they are doing.
- Every day, change the pairings of children so that each infant has this experience with every other child in the room.

Extensions/Modifications

- As an infant becomes more mobile, encourage him to move and practice his new skills.
- Provide toys that make sounds or do something when he interacts with them.

Watching Other Infants

Area: Social Skills

Developmental Objectives

- to promote the development of social awareness
- to promote social responses between infants

Instructions

- Provide space on the floor for infants to play near one another.
- As they kick their legs, vocalize, smile, and laugh in response to one another, call them by name and verbally label what they are feeling or doing.
- Teach infants words for their feelings and interests.

- Respond with words to infant vocalization. For example, if an infant squeals, respond with a word or a short sentence that describes what she may be feeling. "You are excited. You like to see your friends."
- Teach infants that others have the same feelings they do. For example, say, "Margie is excited and kicking her legs" or "Listen to Geno laugh. He feels happy."

Extensions/Modifications

- As infants get older and become curious about other babies, they may poke, pat, push, or mouth another baby. Model for babies how to touch one another. Help them learn the difference between objects and people.

Learning to Relate to and Interact with the Environment

Playing Games

Area: Classroom Community

Developmental Objectives

- to play interactive games with infants in the classroom
- to promote feelings of connectedness in the classroom community

Instructions

- Hold an infant on your lap and play pat-a-cake or peekaboo. Pause and wait for him to respond and then play pat-a-cake or peekaboo again.

- Sit with two infants propped near each other and alternate playing games with them. Encourage them to watch each other.
- Call the infants by name and describe their facial expressions and movements aloud.

Extensions/Modifications

- As infants learn to sit alone, put two of them on the floor and sit nearby. Play pat-a-cake with each child, taking turns.

Singing with Another Infant

Area: Classroom Community

Developmental Objectives

- to provide an opportunity for infants to be near one another
- to promote interaction and feelings of connectedness in the classroom community

Instructions

- Sit on the floor and hold two infants in your lap or place two infants near each other. Sing a song to the babies and encourage them to sing along with you.

- Each day, change the pairings of children so that each infant has this experience with every other child in the room.

Extensions/Modifications

- As two infants learn to sit alone, place them on the floor and sit nearby. Sing, clap your hands, and move to the music.

- Make up songs using the children's names.

Noticing Other Infants

Area: Classroom Community

Developmental Objectives

- to support infants' interest in one another
- to promote feelings of connectedness in the classroom community

Instructions

- Throughout the day, observe the infants when they are watching one another. Encourage infants to notice each other and then describe to each infant what the other one is doing. For example, say, "Jack, you are watching Katy play."
- Describe what infants do in response to each other and talk to each infant about the other. Describe movements, including what each child is doing, what each is seeing, and how they are feeling. For example, "Josie, you are watching Maurice and smiling. You like playing near Maurice." See pages 26–27 for types of descriptions to use with infants.

Infants begin to vocalize to one another as they become more mobile. They watch one another and may smile or laugh in response to another baby. An infant may even begin to prefer the company of a specific baby.

Extensions/Modifications

- When you notice two babies looking at and responding to each other, call each child by name and describe what they are doing.
- If you see that an infant prefers to be close to another baby, place the two close enough so they can watch and make facial expressions at each other.

Making Friends

Area: Classroom Community

Developmental Objectives

- to promote the development of social awareness
- to promote feelings of connectedness in the classroom community

As infants develop more motor control, they may treat other babies as objects—poking, pushing, sitting on them, or crawling over them. Help infants learn respect for one another.

Instructions

- Sit two infants together on the floor. Talk with each of the infants about the other. Call them both by name and introduce them.
- Describe what happens as the infants look at each other. If they make sounds at each other, elaborate on these sounds and tell each what you think the other is trying to communicate.
- Model how to gently touch someone else and describe aloud what you are doing. Take turns with two infants, showing them how to touch each other.

Extensions/Modifications

- Help infants develop empathy and teach them how their behavior affects other children. Use feeling words to describe how one infant's behavior is experienced by another. For example, a child may grab another infant's hair out of curiosity, making her cry. Say, "You wanted to feel Lily's hair. It hurt when you pulled her hair, and she is crying. Use gentle hands to touch Lily's hair." Then model how to touch without hurting.

Looking at Photographs of Works of Art

Area: Broader Community and Society

Developmental Objectives

- to provide cultural art experiences
- to promote feelings of connectedness to the broader community and society

Instructions

- Look for photographs in magazines or other publications that show how families in your area live. Use photographs of art and sculpture that depict the cultures of the children and families in your program.
- With a black marker, write a simple title or one-word description on each photograph and then laminate them. Write these titles in home languages and English.
- Put the photographs together to make a simple book.
- Hold an infant on your lap, point to the pictures, and talk about them. Describe and say the names of things in her home language. For example, if you have a photograph of a red barn, you could say *red* in English and *rojo* in Spanish.

Extensions/Modifications

- Create a wall collage of art where infants and their families can see the photographs.
- Sit with two or more infants and talk with them about the photographs. Call each child by name and encourage the children to interact.

Taking a Tour of Our Building

Area: Broader Community and Society

Developmental Objectives

- to provide an opportunity to explore the building
- to promote feelings of connectedness to the broader school community

Instructions

- Put the infants in strollers and take a tour of the inside of the school building.
- Select one area or room to visit at a time.
- Walk down the hall and look inside rooms as you pass.
- Take the infants on regular tour outings and consider taking them to visit the kitchen, a gym or large room for active indoor play, or other rooms they may not often visit.
- While on the tour, stop often, kneel beside the strollers, and point at what the infants are seeing. Name and talk about objects, people, and things.

Extensions/Modifications

- Visit a group of older children in the building or out on the playground. Let the infants watch the children play.
- Kneel beside the strollers and talk to the infants about what the older children are doing. Let the older children come near, look at, and talk to the babies.

Going for a Walk in a Stroller

Area: Broader Community and Society

Developmental Objectives

- to provide outdoor experiences in the neighborhood
- to promote feelings of connectedness to the broader community

Instructions

- Put the infants in strollers and take a tour of the outside of the building and nearby neighborhood.
- Stop often, kneel beside the strollers, point, and talk with infants. Talk with infants about how the wind feels, what they smell, and what they see.

Extensions/Modifications

- Take walks outside during different seasons of the year.
- Alternate which infants sit together so they all have an opportunity to be near each infant in the group.

Musical Guests

Area: Broader Community and Society

Developmental Objectives

- to provide cultural music experiences
- to promote awareness of different types of music

Instructions

- Invite parents, grandparents, family members, or community members to visit the classroom and play or sing music from their home cultures.
- Ask visitors to sing songs from their childhood, in their home languages.
- Sit on the floor with the infants during the singing and clap and move to the music.
- Record the singers and play the recordings back to the infants at times when you can sit with one or more of them, sing along, clap, and move to the music.

Extensions/Modifications

- Ask families to write down the words to songs from their cultures and send copies home with the infants for singing with families.

Visitors in the Classroom

Area: Broader Community and Society

Developmental Objectives

- to provide experiences with older children from other classrooms
- to promote feelings of connectedness to the broader school community

Instructions

- Invite one or two older children in the program to visit the infant classroom.
- Sit with the older child as you hold an infant on your lap.

- Show the older child how to look at a board book with an infant or show the child how to roll a ball to the infant.
- Take photographs of the visitors and post them on the photo wall.

Extensions/Modifications

- Laminate the photographs taken during the visit onto cardboard and make a simple board book. Sit with an infant on your lap and look at the book. Call people by name

- Never allow older children to pick up, feed, or provide care to infants. The older children may watch as these activities take place to see how infants are cared for in the group setting.

and describe what is happening in each photograph. Make an extra book for the older children who came to visit for them to look at in their classroom.

CHAPTER 6

Social Studies for Infants 8 to 12 Months

The developmental capabilities of infants from eight to twelve months of age provide many opportunities for social-studies learning. These infants are gaining increasing control of their bodies and paying more attention to what people say and do. They begin picking up smaller items with their finger and thumb rather than just raking or grabbing an object into their hand. They may become fearful of strangers and get upset when separated from primary caregivers.

Differing rates of motor development are typical in groups of eight- to twelve-month-old infants. This means that there will be variation in infants' mobility during these months. Some may be crawling or walking, while others of the same age are not. Infants with increased mobility may push other babies' hands away, push them down, or sit on them. This is typical behavior, and it provides an opportunity for you to teach social skills and respect for others. Infants need help in learning how to be around one another, how to touch and interact with one another, and how to respect one another's feelings. Social-studies learning opportunities present themselves on a daily basis in a classroom of eight- to twelve-month-old infants.

For the following activities, make a copy of the Infant-Toddler Social Studies Activity Observation (see appendix H on the Web Components tab at www.redleafpress.org/itss) for each infant. Use the form to record how an infant responds to the activity. Describe how the infant's verbalizations, facial expressions, and body movements change as he develops. Remember that infants and toddlers with developmental delays, disabilities, or other special needs may need individualized adaptations for these activities. Adaptations should be designed and approved by a child's therapists. See page 30 for additional information.

Learning about Oneself

Learning about Myself

Area: Sense of Self

Developmental Objectives

- to promote movement and play
- to promote the development of a positive sense of self

Instructions

- As an infant begins sitting alone, place her in front of an unbreakable mirror that has been securely attached to the wall.
- Sit near her and talk about her reflection in the mirror.
- Reach out and touch your own reflection and then the infant's.
- Point out the baby's facial features in the mirror and encourage her to touch and pat her image in the mirror.

Extensions/Modifications

- Have dolls for infants to play with that reflect the races, ethnicities, and cultures of the children and their families. Sit on the floor with one or more infants and have a doll for each. Point to the doll's eyes, nose, and mouth. Encourage the infants to point at the dolls' body parts. Then point to your own eyes, nose, and mouth. Ask the infants to show you their eyes, nose, and mouth. Repeat the activity using different body parts.

Learning Body Parts

Area: Sense of Self

Developmental Objectives

- to teach the names of body parts
- to promote the development of a positive sense of self

Instructions

- Make up a song to teach parts of the body. A good tune to use is "Here We Go Around the Mulberry Bush."
- As you sit with an infant in front of the mirror, sing the song. "This is the way we touch our mouth, touch our mouth, touch our mouth. This is the way we touch our mouth, early in the morning."

- Go through various body parts.

- Note that infants have a short attention span, so don't make the game too long.

Extensions/Modifications

- As infants learn to sit near other children, play the game with two or more at a time.

Sit together on the floor and sing the song. Encourage the infants to watch each other.

My Body and Clothes

Area: Sense of Self

Developmental Objectives

- to teach the names of body parts and clothing
- to promote the development of a positive sense of self

Instructions

- Use diapering and dressing time to teach infants the names of their body parts and the names of their clothing.
- Describe what you want the child to do and name the body part and piece of clothing in question. For example, say, "This is your T-shirt. It goes over your head. You can help."

- Pause and wait for the child to get ready before beginning to put the shirt over her head.
- Use self-description and child-description (see pages 26–27) to promote communication and language development.

Extensions/Modifications

- It is common for infants to reach for and explore their genitals during diaper changes. Teachers should not shame or scold children for these normal behaviors.

- Teaching young children the correct names of all their body parts helps them develop more positive attitudes about their bodies.

My Special Comfort Item

Area: Sense of Self

Developmental Objectives

- to promote the ability to calm self
- to promote the ability to self-regulate

Instructions

- Encourage families to provide a comfort item for their infant to use during transitions, such as drop-off, or perhaps during naptime.
- Use the child's comfort item during transitional times throughout the day.
- When he begins to calm down, help him get

Learning to engage in play and to entertain themselves helps children begin to regulate their own behavior and to develop motor, communication, and social skills.

interested in play or an interaction with you or another child.

- As you transition him to play, put the comfort item away and out of sight, perhaps in a cubbie or diaper bag.

Extensions/Modifications

- Help infants develop self-regulation skills by teaching them sign language, gestures, and words to express their feelings. Also, give children space to be alone and to calm themselves when needed.

Venturing Out and Exploring

Area: Sense of Self

Developmental Objectives

- to promote feelings of security
- to promote exploration and the development of self-confidence

Instructions

- In the classroom, stay close and be available for infants to crawl to you or reach out and touch you as they become more mobile and begin to move to explore the environment.
- Make eye contact and provide verbal encouragement to help reluctant infants physically move away from you during play.
- Sit on the floor where infants can crawl into your lap and then crawl away.

Extensions/Modifications

- As infants begin to walk, sit in a low chair where they can touch you. As they move away and come back to you, infants build self-confidence in their new abilities while at the same time feeling secure because you are close to help them if needed.

I Can Wait

Area: Sense of Self

Developmental Objectives

- to promote the ability to self-regulate
- to promote language and communication development

Instructions

- Recognize cues that signal what an infant feels and needs. For example, when an infant is hungry and fussing and you are preparing her food, you can say aloud to her that you know she is hungry and that it will be a few minutes until the food is ready.
- Describe what you are doing to get the food prepared and say that you will do it as quickly as possible.

> The needs of young infants should be met as quickly as possible. As infants get older, you can help them begin to learn delay of gratification and self-regulation.

- Follow through quickly and meet the infant's needs.
- Watch for opportunities to use these strategies to help her learn to wait a short period of time.

Extensions/Modifications

- When an infant is in distress and crying, do not use this activity. She has lost the ability to self-regulate at this point, and you should immediately go to her, pick her up, hold her close, and reassure her that she will be okay and that her needs will be met.

Temperament and Motor Skills

Area: Sense of Self

Developmental Objectives

- to promote exploration and motor development
- to promote the development of self-confidence

Instructions

- Think about each infant's temperament styles using the IT3 tool described in appendix A. Assess your own temperament and continue to adapt and plan activities based on individual needs and characteristics.
- An infant who begins to become more mobile and whose temperament is more adventurous needs a safe place to practice new motor skills and to explore. Safety-proof a play space in the classroom where he can be more active and practice new skills. Stay close as he moves around, practices new motor skills, and explores new objects.
- An infant who is more cautious when acquiring new motor skills may need you to scaffold play experiences and encourage him to try new things. For example, a cautious infant may get upset if he falls over while learning to sit alone, roll over, crawl, and pull up. Sit near him and help him stay upright when learning to sit or crawl.

Extensions/Modifications

- Infants who like to watch, make transitions more slowly, and adapt to new people, places, and things over time will need your support and encouragement to move away from you and do more things on their own. Use eye contact and encouragement to help infants who are reluctant to practice new motor skills to begin to do so.

Making Music

Area: Family

Developmental Objectives

- to promote awareness of music
- to promote feelings of belonging to home cultures

Instructions

- Collect safe, age-appropriate musical instruments used in the infants' home cultures, such as bells, chimes, maracas, and drums. Safe teacher-made instruments can also be used.
- Sit on the floor with an infant on your lap and play with the instruments. Encourage her to move her body to the rhythm of the music.
- Sit two infants together and encourage them to play with the musical instruments.
- Show them how to sway with the rhythm of the music they make.

Extensions/Modifications

- Collect music played in infants' home cultures. Play the songs and give infants musical instruments to play along with the music. Encourage them to keep time with the rhythm and beat of the music. Show them how to clap their hands and sway to the music.

Books about Families

Area: Family

Developmental Objectives

- to promote feelings of belonging to a family
- to promote early literacy skills

Instructions

- Collect several sturdy board books about families, such as *Are You My Mother?* by P. D. Eastman. Hold an infant on your lap or sit on the floor with several infants and read the book. Engage the child with the book by pointing to pictures and words and by stopping to ask questions. Talk about mothers, fathers, and families. Encourage the child to point at pictures and to turn the pages.

Extensions/Modifications

- Collect books about families and put them in a plastic bin on the floor for infants to explore independently. Be alert to infants' interest in the books and sit with them to read the books over and over.

Family Dolls

Area: Family

Developmental Objectives

- to promote feelings of belonging to a family
- to provide play experiences with dolls

Instructions

- Collect safe, soft dolls of children, mothers, fathers, and grandparents. If you are unable to find them, you can make simple dolls from fabric, such as muslin, filled with soft stuffing. Draw faces and hair on the dolls using safe fabric crayons (see instructions on the crayon box) or sew features on with thread that is securely attached so they do not present a choking hazard. Make dolls from different colors for a variety of skin tones.
- Sit with one or more infants and play with the dolls. Talk about families and name the dolls. For example, say, "This is the daddy doll." Act out pretend activities: "Mommy is going to work. She is waving bye-bye."

Extensions/Modifications

- Make simple doll furniture to use with the family dolls. Use a shoe box for a bed and make a small pillow and blanket. Sit with one or more infants and play with the family dolls, acting out going to bed.

Our Families

Area: Family

Developmental Objectives

- to promote feelings of belonging to a family
- to promote the development of social awareness

Instructions

- As infants grow and develop, take photographs periodically of them with their families.
- Create a display in the room so that families and infants can see themselves as they arrive and leave each day.
- Make a collage of the family photographs on poster board and cover it with clear contact paper or laminate it.
- Put the collage on a wall close to the floor where infants can see it as they play.
- Talk with infants about the families and describe the people in the photographs to the infants. For example, say, "That is Theresa's father," as you point to a picture.
- Point out the infant's own family and family members.

Extensions/Modifications

- Create a welcoming area for families that reflects the diversity of families in your classroom and the community. Display photographs that are representative of all types of diversity—including race, ethnicity, and family configurations such as same-sex parents or grandparents as primary caregivers.
- Cut pictures from magazines and laminate them to make family picture cards or books.

My Family Caregiver

Area: Family

Developmental Objectives

- to promote attachment to home caregivers
- to promote the development of trust and feelings of security

Instructions

- Take photographs of an infant with the family members who bring and pick up the child from care each day.
- Write the infant's name and the names of his family members on the photographs.
- Laminate the photographs onto sturdy cardboard and make a simple book.
- Hold him on your lap or sit on the floor with the child after he is dropped off for the day. Look at his book and talk about how his family members come back to get him.
- Point to the photographs and call people by name.

Extensions/Modifications

- Sit with two or more infants and look at their family photo books. Talk with them and show each the other's family photos. Talk about families.

Learning to Relate to and Interact with Other People

Playing Close to Another Baby

Area: Social Skills

Developmental Objectives

- to promote the development of social awareness
- to promote the ability to play near others

Instructions

- As infants become more mobile, put two babies on the floor together to watch each other as they play.

Do not label babies with such words as *shy* or *wild* or any description based on your perception of a child's behavior, temperament, or personality. A label can become a self-fulfilling prophecy where a child begins to exhibit the characteristics that the label implies.

- Allow them to watch each other as they sit, roll, crawl, or pull up.
- Draw the infants' attention to each other. Call them by name and describe to each baby what the other is doing.

- Describe their watching of each other. Talk with each baby about their feelings and experiences.
- Talk about how the children are different and how they are alike. Make it okay not to be like everyone else.

Extensions/Modifications

- See and respect each child as an individual who is capable and whose characteristics add value to the social group. Help children feel good about themselves by providing them opportunities to feel connected and important in the classroom community. Give special attention to the infant who is quiet and perhaps more unsure or hesitant to play or interact. Hold her on your lap and sit on the floor near other infants. Help her feel connected by describing what the other children are doing. Say, "Jenny is watching you play. Come over and say hello to Jenny." It may take time for the child to feel comfortable and begin to connect and interact.

Singing and Doing Finger Plays

Area: Social Skills

Developmental Objectives

- to promote awareness of music
- to promote play and social development

Instructions

- Sit on the floor with two infants and model how to sit together and play.
- Sing simple songs or rhymes and do simple finger plays. For example, sing a name song to the tune of "Are You Sleeping?" Sing, "Where is Maria? Where is Maria? Here I am. Here I am."
- Take turns with the infants, involving them both in the play.

- Call each child by name as you play and sing.
- Model how to be near each other, how to touch each other, and how to crawl or walk around each other.
- Use child descriptions (see page 27) to talk to them about how they are experiencing the game or interaction together.

Extensions/Modifications

- Each day, have different infants sit and play near each other so they become familiar with all children in the classroom. Call each child by name and teach them the others' names.

Playing with the Same Toys

Area: Social Skills

Developmental Objectives

- to promote the ability to sit near and play with similar toys
- to promote the development of social skills

Instructions

- Sit with two infants and give them each a plastic bucket or other container that has toy animals or other play objects inside.
- Show the infants how to dump out the bucket and to put its contents back in again.
- Sit near and describe what they are doing using words such as *in*, *out*, and *over*.
- Help the infants sit near and watch each other. Call them both by name and describe what they are doing.

Extensions/Modifications

- Model words such as *please* and *thank you* as you and the infants take turns playing with the containers and toys. Use the types of talk on pages 26–27 as the infants play.

Crawling around Together

Area: Social Skills

Developmental Objectives

- to promote active play with another infant
- to promote the development of social skills

Instructions

- As infants begin to crawl, place a sturdy box or make a simple tent that they can crawl into. Play the going away and coming back game as they crawl into the space and cannot be seen. Sit near and describe what they are doing.
- Model for two infants how to crawl into the box or tent and sit together. Sit near and describe what's happening using words such as *in*, *out*, and *under*. Use words such as *together* and *sitting close*. Call each infant by name.

Extensions/Modifications

- Sit with two infants who have learned to pull up and encourage them to pull up to the same table. Have some soft toys ready on top of the table. Show them how to pat the table or bang on it with a toy. Model for the infants and encourage them to repeat your actions. Draw their attention to each other, call them by name, and describe their play.

Peekaboo

Area: Social Skills

Developmental Objectives

- to promote the development of social skills
- to promote turn-taking and interactions with others

Instructions

- Play peekaboo with one or more infants.
- Say, "I'm going away," and hide your face with a scarf or small piece of cloth. Then take the scarf away from your face and say, "I came back."
- Encourage the infants to play the game by holding the scarf in front of their faces in turn.

- Call each baby by name as you play the game. Say, "Where did Isabel go?" Then say, "I'm glad Isabel came back."
- Describe using self-talk and parallel talk (see page 27) to make the game meaningful in building relationships between the infants.

Extensions/Modifications

- Cover a doll or stuffed animal with a small soft cloth. Say, "Where did bear go?" Then raise the cloth and say, "Peekaboo!"

Encourage the children to put the cloth over a toy and to pull it off.

Using Gestures to Communicate

Area: Communication

Developmental Objectives

- to promote language and communication development
- to notice and respect infant cues

Instructions

- Respond to an infant's nonverbal communication with words.
- Imitate the sounds that infants make and then expand and elaborate on these sounds by responding with words. For example, an infant may signal that she is finished eating

> Mealtime provides an opportunity to support infants' communication and language development. They use gestures and sounds to communicate when they are hungry, full, or enjoying their food.

through cues such as shaking her head, clamping her mouth shut, or dropping food on the floor. You can say aloud, "You are all done" or "You are full. Let's clean up." Repeat "all done" or "full" several times so she begins to learn a word to communicate she does not want more food.

Extensions/Modifications

- Learn baby sign language and teach infants to sign things such as *all done*, *please*, *more*, or *sleepy*. Information about baby sign language is available online, and many sites include illustrations or video clips to teach you how to do it.

- Use the different types of descriptive talk on pages 26–27 during routines and play times to help infants hear words and learn language.

Learning Words for Feelings

Area: Communication

Developmental Objectives

- to promote language and communication development
- to promote the ability to use words to express feelings

Instructions

- Cut pictures from magazines of people's facial expressions.
- Laminate the photographs on heavy cardboard and make a simple feelings book.
- Sit with an infant and look at the feelings book.
- Wait for him to look, point, and make his own facial expression and sounds.

- Point to the faces and facial features in the picture and name the feeling that the person is exhibiting, such as, "She is happy. See her big smile?"
- Teach words for different feelings, such as *mad*, *sad*, *afraid*, *excited*, and *frustrated*.

Extensions/Modifications

- Teach infants how to use baby sign language to communicate their feelings. Teach them how to sign *happy*, *sad*, *afraid*, *mad*, and other feeling words. Use baby sign language in conjunction with verbal language to describe what a child may be feeling as well as your own feelings.

Looking at Books

Area: Communication

Developmental Objectives

- to promote interest in books
- to promote language and communication development

Instructions

- Put sturdy picture books in an area where infants can reach and look at them independently.
- Sit with an infant and look at the books with her.
- Point to and talk about the pictures in a book.

- Use gestures, sounds, and different tones of voice while reading aloud to make the book interesting.
- Include books that feature people of different ages, races, and ethnicities.
- Include books that picture common objects from the children's home cultures.

Extensions/Modifications

- Observe what types of books and stories an infant seems to enjoy. Repeatedly read these favorite books to him. Individualize your interactions based on his interests and enjoyment. Collect books in infants' home languages and read them, if possible.
- Learn some common words in an infant's home language and use them as you look at books with the child.

Watching and Hearing

Area: Communication

Developmental Objectives

- to promote language and communication development
- to promote interest and engagement during daily routines

Instructions

- Use the different types of description presented on pages 26–27 to talk with infants and help them learn new words. For example, use self-description by making eye contact with an infant and then verbally telling her what you are doing. Point to and name the objects and tools you are using. Pause and give her time to think and respond. You might say, "You are watching me wipe off the table. You are interested in what I am doing. See the cloth? It is wet and I'm cleaning the table for lunch."

- Using different types of description is a learning strategy you can use throughout the day during caregiving routines and play experiences.

Extensions/Modifications

- Look for opportunities for infants to watch people do new things and opportunities to hear new words—for example, looking out of a window as the garbage truck picks up the garbage.

Learning Animal Names and Sounds

Area: Communication

Developmental Objectives

- to promote language and communication development
- to promote singing and play

Instructions

- Sit on the floor with two or more infants and several stuffed animals or soft plastic animals.
- Sing "Old MacDonald" with the infants.
- Name each animal and make the sound the animal makes as you sing the song.
- Pause when singing and wait for the babies to make sounds.
- Act out animals running or jumping.
- Encourage the infants to interact with the toy animals and make sounds.

Extensions/Modifications

- As the infants learn the animals and their sounds, add more stuffed animals to the game.
- Learn the names of animals in a child's home language and sing the song using these names.

Learning to Relate to and Interact with the Environment

Exploring Textures

Area: Classroom Community

Developmental Objectives

- to promote tactile learning experiences in the classroom environment
- to promote exploration

Instructions

- Using nontoxic glue, cover cardboard squares with different textured materials, such as sandpaper, velvet, corduroy, fluffy fleece, and satin.
- Punch holes along one edge of each square and ring them together to make a touch book.
- Make several books with different textures and colors of materials.
- Make books with two contrasting materials on each page or cut small shapes out of the background material and glue contrasting texture in the space.

Infants' temperament styles influence how they interact with and experience the environment around them. Providing infants with tactile experiences while being observant and sensitive to their individual reactions can help to inform your planning, care, and teaching.

- Sit with an infant and show him the book. Show him how to feel the pages as you talk about what he feels.
- Use descriptive words such as *rough*, *smooth*, *soft*, *shiny*, and *ridges*.
- Place the books on a low shelf, in a container, or on the floor where infants can hold and explore them on their own. The children will put books in their mouths, so make sure there are no loose pieces. Discard books as they become worn.

Extensions/Modifications

- Sit with two babies and look at the touch books together. Call each infant by name and encourage them to let each other feel a page in both books. Use child description (see page 27).
- Ask, "May I touch your book?" Pause and wait for the child to indicate a response.

Teach babies sign language, words, and gestures to communicate yes or no. Touch a page in the baby's book and talk about how it feels. Say, "Thank you for letting me touch the page."

Making Music

Area: Classroom Community

Developmental Objectives

- to promote awareness of different types of music and musical instruments
- to provide an opportunity for infants to make music together
- to promote the feeling of community within the classroom environment

Instructions

- Sit on the floor with two or more infants and musical instruments like those used in the infants' home cultures, such as bells, chimes, maracas, and drums.
- Model how to make music and sing together. Allow room for the children to move to the music.

- Call each child by name and describe what he is doing with his instrument. "Jack is ringing a bell. Listen. Hear the bell?"
- Describe their facial expressions. Use self-talk and parallel talk (see page 27) to help infants notice other babies in the group.

Extensions/Modifications

- Put the music-makers where the infants can play with them on their own.
- Play music and encourage the babies to play along with their instruments.

- Model how to move to music and encourage the infants to do the same.
- Include recorded music that is representative of the infants' home cultures.

Eating Together

Area: Classroom Community

Developmental Objectives

- to promote feelings of connectedness to others
- to promote positive mealtime experiences
- to promote the development of social skills

> Social, communication, motor, and self-help skills are enhanced when teachers model, describe, and scaffold learning experiences during snacks and meals.

Instructions

- Place infants where they can see one another as they eat. If they are fed in high chairs, place the chairs in a small circle.
- Sit and eat with them.
- Call each baby by name and talk about what each is eating and doing. This is a social

time when infants can feel part of the classroom family.
- When babies are able to sit in small chairs at a low table, several of them can sit together for snacks and meals.

Extensions/Modifications

- Expect spills and accidents during meals. This is an opportunity to teach self-regulation, verbal communication, and problem solving. Model emotional control and how to handle accidents when they occur. Infants will learn what people do when they are angry, frustrated, and impatient by watching and modeling what you do and say. Verbally explain what has happened and what you are going to do. For example, say, "Oh, I spilled the juice. I am going to get a cloth and wipe it up." You model that it is okay. Acknowledge mistakes or accidents when they happen and model what you want the infants to learn to do.

Dropping Objects

Area: Classroom Community

Developmental Objectives

- to provide learning experiences that match interest and developmental needs
- to promote feelings of competence within the classroom community

Instructions

- When an infant begins to take an interest in dropping things and watching them fall, design learning opportunities for her to experiment with dropping when she is not eating.
- Show her how to sit on a safe-size infant chair and drop objects such as soft blocks or small balls into a plastic laundry basket or empty shoe box.
- Describe what happens as the child drops objects. For example, say, "When you drop the block, it goes down."

Infants' behavior is driven by the desire to become competent, to learn about the world, and to know what they can do with their bodies. These behaviors are not misbehaviors but are signs of exploration and learning. One behavior that you may observe at this age—or earlier—is an infant intentionally dropping things (including food) off her high chair or the table. Remember that she is learning about the world; this includes cause and effect and how gravity works.

- She can also sit on the floor and drop a toy into a bucket or container.

Extensions/Modifications

- You can design safe opportunities for infants to practice climbing and to do other motor activities that they are compelled to do as they strive to learn about themselves and the environment.

Exploring the Neighborhood

Area: Broader Community and Society

Developmental Objectives

- to promote awareness of the neighborhood and outdoors
- to promote feelings of connectedness to the broader community

Instructions

- Take infants for stroller walks outside.
- As you walk, stop often, kneel down, and talk to the infants about what you are seeing.
- Take photographs as you walk that include the infants and the things they see.
- Print the photographs and laminate them on cardboard.
- Put the photos in a sequence. You might begin with a photo showing the infants getting ready to go, then one in the strollers, one in the hall, and one going outside. Punch holes in the side of the photos and put them together with rings.
- Sit with one or more infants and look at the book. Talk about and describe each photo, saying things like "First, you put on your coat and hat."
- Call infants by name as you point to and talk about their images in the photographs.

Extensions/Modifications

- Put the photographs on the wall where infants can look at them while they are playing on the floor. Talk with the infants about the experience.

Community Celebrations

Area: Broader Community and Society

Developmental Objectives

- to promote feelings of connectedness to the broader community
- to promote partnership with families

Instructions

- Ask families to bring photographs of their family and community celebrations.
- Print and laminate the photographs to make a picture wall or book.
- Sit with one or more infants and point at the things you see in the photographs. Call family members by name and describe what they are doing in the photographs.

Extensions/Modifications

- Cut pictures from magazines and publications that depict people at community and cultural celebrations and events. Include photographs of people of differing abilities, races, ages, and ethnicities. Laminate photographs onto sturdy cardboard and make board books for the infants to explore.

Our Community

Area: Broader Community and Society

Developmental Objectives

- to promote feelings of connectedness to the broader community
- to promote language development

Instructions

- Take photographs of city buildings, parks, grocery stores, and schools in your community. If you live in a rural area, take photographs of local landmarks such as grain elevators, fields of corn, and farmhouses. Include photographs of places that families may visit. Print the photographs to make posters. Label each poster. Put the posters on the wall at infants' eye level so they can see the pictures when they are playing on the floor. Talk with the infants about what they see in each poster.

Extensions/Modifications

- Print smaller photographs of the community, laminate them, and make board books for the infants to explore independently. Sit with one or more infants, look at the books, and point at and name the things you see in the photographs.

Community Workers

Area: Broader Community and Society

Developmental Objectives

- to promote feelings of connectedness to the broader community
- to promote early literacy skills

Instructions

- Find photographs of community workers and helpers such as firefighters, police officers, garbage truck drivers, postal workers, doctors, nurses, and so on in magazines and other publications. Make sure that the photographs depict people of different races, ethnicities, genders, and abilities. Label and laminate the photographs onto sturdy cardboard. Make board books for the infants to explore. Sit and talk with them about community workers and what they do. Point to the pictures and engage the infants with the books.

Extensions/Modifications

- Put the board books in a bin on the floor for infants to explore independently. Find and make available books that feature different types of work and workers that help people in communities. Two good examples are *Katy and the Big Snow* and *Mike Mulligan and His Steam Shovel*, both by Virginia Lee Burton.

Social Studies for Toddlers 12 to 18 Months

As infants become toddlers, they want to be independent and have autonomy. These developmental tasks build on the feelings of trust and security that infants and toddlers develop with primary caregivers and on advancements in their motor and cognitive skills. Motor skills that develop during the second year of life include the ability to walk, climb, open, close, pull, push, hold, and drop objects. Toddlers' social-emotional development includes the feeling of pride in the accomplishments of new motor skills. They want to practice these new skills and do things by themselves. They watch and imitate family members and other adults in an effort to learn the skills that are important for participation in their culture and community. From twelve to eighteen months, toddlers are gaining control of their bodies and using new motor skills to learn self-help skills and to do things for themselves. They are physically active, exploring, experimenting, listening, and watching everything. They begin to talk and to communicate verbally and with gestures. Their receptive language—what they hear and understand—increases, and they understand more than they can say themselves. They like to be around and watch other babies but need help learning how to touch and interact with one another.

By twelve months of age, some babies stand alone and may be taking a few steps. Other twelve-month-olds may even be walking well on their own. The range of age for walking can be anywhere from eight to eighteen months. Children's individual rates of development, temperaments and personalities, family expectations, and culture, as well as other factors, affect when they start walking. As toddlers begin to walk, their language development may temporarily take a backseat.

Toddlers jabber and make sounds that are word-like. They still use gestures to communicate. They may say "bye-bye" or other familiar words, combining them with a hand wave. Children this age like to play simple games like peekaboo, and they can roll a ball back and forth with another person. Some may be walking well and be able to bend over from a standing position and pick something up, and they may try to lift heavy objects. Toddlers are refining their abilities to drink from cups and to feed themselves with spoons.

By fourteen months, toddlers are usually walking to get from one place to another. They like to push and pull toys while walking and will imitate behaviors, such as mowing the lawn or running the vacuum, with toy replicas. Toddlers this age can point to one or more body parts when asked and can follow other simple requests. They finger-feed, use spoons and forks, and drink from cups. Simple games are enjoyable for them, so many will initiate playing these games on their own. They can match items that go together, such as the lid that goes on a pot. They like to empty the contents of containers and to take toys apart.

Motor skills increase by fifteen months, and toddlers may begin to run, walk upstairs, walk backward, and play with balls. They want to help adults do things and to try out the things they see others do. They like to scribble with crayons and draw lines. As their motor skills become more refined, they begin to concentrate on learning words and increasing their vocabularies. Though they understand what others say and may be able to say five or more words themselves, they continue to use gestures and imitate the gestures of others.

Toddlers are interested in books and by sixteen months can turn pages themselves. Many are able to stack two or three blocks. Because they are learning independence by trying to do things by themselves, they may have mastered some new skills, such as taking off pieces of their own clothing. Tantrums are not uncommon, especially when the child is tired or frustrated. Toddlers also begin to show food preferences and may resist some kinds of food. A toddler is also fascinated by how things work. There is an increased desire to learn the correct way to use common objects like phones, TV remotes, and so on, by watching how others use these objects.

At seventeen months, some toddlers' words become clearer, and they may be saying and using several words on a regular basis. They understand and respond to verbal instructions and are better able to follow directions. Toddlers like to sort toys and can learn to do so by size, color, and shape. Music, singing, dancing, and simple movement games are fun for toddlers. During this time, as toddlers begin to experience a more active lifestyle, you should plan and create safe opportunities for active play. Riding toys, kicking balls, dancing, and participating in pretend games (especially if adults model and interact with them in pretend play), are some enjoyable activities for this age group.

For the following activities, make a copy of the Infant-Toddler Social Studies Activity Observation (see appendix H on the Web Components tab at www .redleafpress.org/itss) for each toddler. Use the form to record how a toddler responds to the activity. Describe how the toddler's verbalizations, facial expressions, and body movements change as she develops. Remember that infants and toddlers with developmental delays, disabilities, or other special needs may need individualized adaptations for these activities. Adaptations should be designed and approved by a child's therapists. See page 30 for additional information.

Learning about Oneself

Learning to Do Things

Area: Sense of Self

Developmental Objectives

- to promote the development of a positive sense of self
- to promote the development of motor skills

Instructions

- Take photographs of a toddler playing and doing things in the classroom.
- Print the photographs on card stock.
- Write the child's name on her photo card.
- Sit with her and talk about her photographs, describing what she is doing.

Extensions/Modifications

- Make postcards from the photographs to send home to each toddler's family. Write messages on the back of the postcards. Use the postcards as a way to inform families about development and to provide examples of how their children learn through play.
- Make more family postcards but leave the backs blank. Send home several postcards with each toddler. Encourage the families to return the postcards with a written message that can be read to their children during the day. Sit with a toddler and read her family's message.
- Make a collage display on a bulletin board or on the wall low enough for toddlers to see. Talk with the children about their photographs.
- Save the postcards and give them back to families as you take new photographs, showing toddlers' growth, development, and learning.

A Place for My Things

Area: Sense of Self

Developmental Objectives

- to promote the development of a positive sense of self
- to promote feelings of security and belonging

Instructions

- Make a space for each child to keep personal things. Take photographs of the children and write their names on them. Laminate or cover the photographs with clear contact paper. Put each child's photograph on a separate cubbie, plastic bin, or sturdy box. Place the cubbies, bins, or boxes where toddlers can reach them. Help a toddler find his cubbie by looking at and talking about his photograph and pointing to his name. Put photographs of the children's families inside their cubbies.
- Encourage the toddlers to get their coats and hats from their cubbies when going outside and to hang them up when they come back. Say things like, "You did it. You got your coat and hat."
- Use cubbies for storing the toddlers' extra clothes, items to send home, and so on.

Extensions/Modifications

- Play a game with the toddlers by asking "Whose cubbie is this?" Help them learn one another's names and how to recognize other toddlers from their photographs.

Doing Things and Feeling Competent

Area: Sense of Self

Developmental Objectives

- to promote feelings of competence
- to promote the development of a positive sense of self

Instructions

- Toddlers want to learn how to do things they see adults do. Collect several small shoe boxes, empty clean round oatmeal boxes, yogurt containers with lids, and clean plastic jars with lids. Put a toy that is large enough not to be a choking hazard inside each box or jar. Safe plastic toy foods would be good to use. Put the lids on the boxes and jars and place them in a plastic bin or plastic laundry basket. Note that removing the lids requires different techniques. Box lids lift off, yogurt container lids snap off, and jar lids screw off. You can start with one type of lid and then add different types of containers as toddlers gain skills. Change out the toys to present new experiences.

- Sit on the floor with a toddler and the basket of boxes and jars. Take the lid off of one. Describe what you are doing with words such as *off*, *in*, and *on* as you take lids off, look inside, name the toy, and put the lid back on. Encourage the toddler to do this by herself. Continue to describe her actions as she plays. Scaffold the activity as needed. For example, she may not be able to unscrew a jar lid. Or she may not be able to put a shoe box lid back on the box. You can assist as needed and as wanted by each toddler.

Extensions/Modifications

- Encourage two or more toddlers to play with the boxes or other containers side by side. Stay close and describe what each toddler does. Call each child by name.

- Learn the words and names of the toys in a child's home language and use these during the game.

Learning about My Emotions

Area: Sense of Self

Developmental Objectives

- to promote the ability to self-regulate
- to learn to express emotions with words

Instructions

- Toddlers have a need to be independent and to begin to do things for themselves. They also experience strong emotions but may not have yet learned how to express these feelings with words. The gestures, facial expressions, and body language that toddlers use are cues to their feelings and their needs. Do not shame toddlers or try to make them feel guilty when they express strong emotions or even lose control and have a tantrum. Instead, model how to handle anger, frustration, and disappointment for them. Think about what social-emotional skills you want toddlers to develop and what types of adults you hope they eventually will grow to be. Your teaching is powerful.

- Use self-talk and say aloud how you are feeling when you accidentally drop the finger paints on the floor or spill or knock over something while you're eating or when things do not go as planned. Toddlers are watching and learning from you how they should behave and how they should express their feelings. Teach toddlers socially appropriate and healthy ways to deal with strong emotions.

Extensions/Modifications

- As you look at books with toddlers, talk about how the people in the story are feeling. Point to their faces and talk about what is happening, especially when there is a problem or strong emotions are being expressed. Use words to describe what the people are feeling. Look for simple books that show people having different experiences.

Learning about Myself

Area: Sense of Self

Developmental Objectives

- to promote self-awareness and individual characteristics
- to promote the development of a positive sense of self

Instructions

- Have a variety of dolls with different skin tones, types of hair, and facial features. Sit on the floor near a toddler and pretend with the doll. Pretend that the doll is hungry, sleepy, or upset and crying. Use words to describe how the doll is feeling. Model what the doll can do to help it feel better. Say aloud what can be done to help the doll.
- Use the doll to help the toddler recognize feelings and teach words to express them. For example, say, "You are tired and crying. Let's get your favorite blanket." Use a doll-size blanket and hold it and the doll in your arms. Then say, "It is your naptime."
- Model and use words to help the toddler learn how to get her needs met. For example, pretend the doll is yelling and say, "You want my attention. Use your words and say, 'I need you.'"

Extensions/Modifications

- Sit with two or more toddlers and encourage them to each take care of a doll. Use verbal descriptions as the toddlers play with the dolls.
- Toddlers may hold a comfort item such as a blanket or stuffed toy or suck their thumbs to calm themselves down.
- Notice when one toddler helps or comforts another and describe what happened. For example, "You saw that Jack was upset. You patted Jack on the arm to help him feel better." Do the same when one toddler notices that another child is in distress. "You were watching Maria because she was crying. You knew that she bumped her head and got hurt."

Feelings

Area: Sense of Self

Developmental Objectives

- to promote awareness of feelings
- to promote the ability to self-regulate

Instructions

- Sit with one or more toddlers and use hand puppets to act out feelings and social situations, such as two toddlers wanting the same toy.
- Model what to say and do. Make up pretend scenarios but also act out things that may have occurred in the classroom. Talk for each puppet and describe what is happening and how each puppet feels. Teach toddlers that other people have feelings and their own perceptions of events.

Extensions/Modifications

- With the puppets or dolls, model how a toddler might self-regulate: by going someplace else to play, by getting a book to look at, or by going to a quiet area of the room and holding a stuffed toy until she has quieted down and is ready to rejoin the group.

A Book about What I Can Do

Area: Sense of Self

Developmental Objectives

- to recognize growing motor development and new skills
- to promote the development of a positive sense of self

Instructions

- Toddlers are growing and changing quickly. Make a book for a toddler every few months as he gains new skills. Take photographs of him playing, eating, walking, and doing new things. Label the photographs and laminate onto cardboard. Punch holes in the side and attach the pages with rings or tightly tied string to make a book.
- Sit with the toddler and look at his book. Talk about what he is doing in the photographs and how he is feeling.
- Give the older books to families as you make new ones.

Extensions/Modifications

- Sit with two or more toddlers and look at their books. Talk about how they are different and how they are alike.
- Toddlers differ in how they show their emotions, how they interact with other people, how they react to new experiences, and how physically active they are. Some toddlers may show fear of new people and experiences. Fearful toddlers may hide or try to move away. Anger or frustration come more frequently to some toddlers than others. They may protest loudly when they are upset. Some toddlers prefer to be alone, and others like to be around other toddlers. The amount of activity toddlers engage in also varies, with some being very energetic and moving all the time, while others are more placid and not as active.
- Be aware of individual differences in children's reactions to daily activities and experiences. Have consistent, predictable routines and help toddlers learn ways to transition from one activity to the next. Alternate active and quiet times to give toddlers time to rest and to move. Give toddlers time to finish what they are doing before starting something new.

Imitating Family Activities

Area: Family

Developmental Objectives

- to provide opportunities to practice skills toddlers see family members doing
- to promote connections between families and the classroom

Instructions

- Toddlers observe and imitate what family members and others do—such as pushing a shopping cart, a baby stroller, or a lawn mower. Toddlers like to push things. Provide small push toys that toddlers can push around the room as they begin to walk.
- Get two or more toddler-size toy shopping carts and fill them with clean, empty food boxes and objects like the ones used in toddlers' homes. Use packages with labels in the children's home languages.
- If empty food boxes are not available, pictures from magazines or newspaper food ads can be cut out, glued onto small boxes and containers, and covered with clear contact paper. Note that some toddlers continue to mouth objects, so supervise toddlers and use nontoxic glue and materials when making toys.
- Talk with the toddlers and point, name, and describe what the "food" items are. Talk with them about what they eat at home. Place the boxes on low shelves and pretend to shop with the children. Encourage two toddlers to "shop" together and to push their baskets around together.
- Provide small, doll-size strollers and dolls for toddlers to push around.

Extensions/Modifications

- Provide push toys for outdoor play. For example, have two or more toy lawn mowers or wheelbarrows for the toddlers to push around during outside play. Add small wagons that the toddlers can pull as they develop motor skills.

- Give the toddlers large soft blocks to put in the wheelbarrows.
- Have large plastic animals for outdoor play that the toddlers can put in wagons and pull around.

Cooking

Area: Family

Developmental Objectives

- to provide opportunities for pretend play
- to promote connections between families and the classroom

Instructions

- Collect realistic, safe, toddler-size kitchen items, such as pots, pans, lids, wooden spoons, spatulas, and food containers. Sit up a play area with a toddler-size refrigerator, stove, sink, table, and chairs. Ask the toddlers what they eat at home or ask their parents. Collect food boxes that are representative of the food the toddlers eat at home and encourage them to pretend to cook it.
- For example, model how to pretend to fry an egg or stir a bowl of cake batter.

Extensions/Modifications

- Collect clean, small plastic jars with lids. Punch holes in the lids. Infuse cotton balls with the scents of common spices that the toddlers' families use in cooking. For example, put a drop of vanilla on a cotton ball or lightly dust one with ground ginger. Some common herbs and spices families may use are cinnamon, nutmeg, cumin, basil, and oregano. Put the cotton balls in the jars and secure the lids with glue. Talk with the toddlers about the different smells and put the jars in the cooking area for the toddlers to use. Be sure to check with families about children's food allergies.

Area: Family

Developmental Objectives

- to provide opportunities to look at books about families and family members
- to promote connections between families and the classroom

Instructions

- Collect books about families and family members, such as *Families* by Rena D. Grossman, *Daddy Makes the Best Spaghetti* by Anna Grossnickle Hines, *Mommies Say Shhh!* by Patricia Polacco, *Global Babies*, by the Global Fund for Children, and *Big Sister and Little Sister* by Charlotte Zolotow. Sit with one or two toddlers, look at the books, and talk about families. Point to pictures in the stories and ask the toddlers questions about what they see. Talk with the toddlers about their own families and the families in the books.

Extensions/Modifications

- Take new pictures of the toddlers' family members and make a family picture book for each child. Update the family books on a regular basis, adding new photographs to reflect the birth of a new sibling or the addition of a grandmother moving in with the family. Sit with the toddlers and look at their family picture books. Put each toddler's book in her cubbie where she can get it and look at when she wants.

Learning to Relate to and Interact with Other People

Area: Communication

Developmental Objectives

- to promote language and communication development
- to promote social interactions

Instructions

- Throughout the day, point at and name objects, food, toys, and people for the toddlers. Toddlers may gesture, point, shake their heads, hold out their arms, and make facial expressions to communicate.

- Respond to toddlers' nonverbal communication with words.
- Do not overwhelm toddlers with talk but do talk often, using different types of description for toddlers to imitate. See page 27 for description examples.
- Learn the names of foods in the children's home languages and use them when talking with the toddlers about the food they are eating.

Extensions/Modifications

- Cut pictures of common objects, food, animals, toys, and household items out of magazines. Laminate the pictures onto heavy cardboard to make picture cards. Make sets of cards using different categories of things. Sit with a toddler as he looks at a set of the cards. Point to the picture on each card, name the item, and talk with the child about it. See if he says the name of the item. Put the picture cards in a box or small container that toddlers can reach.

Learning the Names of Things

Area: Communication

Developmental Objectives

- to promote language and communication development
- to promote social interactions

Instructions

- Use a hand puppet or stuffed animal to play a naming game with one or more toddlers.
- Have the puppet ask each toddler, "What is your name?" Pause and wait for the child to respond. If she does not answer, say for her, "My name is ____?"
- Have the puppet ask other questions such as "What are those?" and point to the child's hands or feet. Wait for her to answer and then answer for her if she does not.

Extensions/Modifications

- Encourage two or more toddlers to sit together as you play the game with them. Call each child by name.

Playing a Naming Game

Area: Communication

Developmental Objectives

- to promote language and communication development
- to promote social interactions

Instructions

- Use a puppet and play a game with a basket of common items or toys.
- Pretend that the puppet does not know what the toys are. Have the puppet pick up a toy and say, "What is this? This looks fun. What is it?"

- Name the item for the toddler and describe it: "This is a block. It feels hard." Add more descriptive words as the children's language skills advance.

Extensions/Modifications

- Encourage two or more toddlers to sit together as you play the game with them. Call each child by name. Encourage them to take turns.

- Learn the names of toys and items in a child's home language and use them during the game.

Looking at Books

Area: Communication

Developmental Objectives

- to provide experiences with books
- to promote the development of early literacy skills
- to promote language and communication development

Instructions

- Collect several large, sturdy picture books.
- Sit with a toddler on your lap and look at a big picture book.
- Name an object on each page and ask the toddler where it is.
- Pause and wait to see if he points to the object. If he does not, point to the object yourself and say what it is.

- If the child points at something different, say what that object is and then point to the one you named.
- Continue this game with the toddler as you go through the book. Allow the child to come and go and do not force him to participate.

Extensions/Modifications

- Encourage two toddlers to sit near each other as the three of you look at the book and play the game.
- As the toddlers learn the names of more things, begin to add descriptive words: "Where is the red hat?"

- Point to multiple objects on a page and count them out loud. Say, "I see one, two, three puppies," touching each puppy with your finger as you count.

Learning to Say Please and Thank You

Area: Social Skills

Developmental Objectives

- to introduce and practice the use of social phrases
- to promote the development of social skills

Instructions

- Social phrases that govern adult interactions can be used with toddlers to help them learn how to conduct themselves in social situations. Model social phrases during interactions with toddlers and other adults by saying aloud "thank you," "please," "I'm sorry," and other things throughout the day.

Toddlers will begin to learn and use these words and phrases, modeling what you do and say.

- Learn social phrases in the toddlers' home languages and use them as you interact with the children and others.

Extensions/Modifications

- Observe the toddlers and document when they begin to use the modeled words and phrases in their own social interactions.

These types of observations and documentation provide evidence of growing social skills and development.

Looking at a Book with Another Toddler

Area: Social Skills

Developmental Objectives

- to promote social interaction
- to promote the development of social skills

Instructions

- Sit on the floor with two or more toddlers and look at a sturdy picture book together. Point to and talk about the pictures in the book. Use gestures and sounds, tone of voice, and changes in volume to make the book interesting.
- Encourage the toddlers to sit near one another and to point and talk about the pictures.

Extensions/Modifications

- Sit on the floor in an area where toddlers are playing. Look at books with one or more toddlers as they come and go around you.

- As the toddlers' attention spans increase, add books with longer stories. Books with rhyming words and repetition are especially enjoyable for toddlers. Read these books over and over to help the toddlers begin to remember the rhymes and repetitions. These types of activities are preliteracy skills and steps in learning to read.

Let the toddlers decide if they want to look at the book or to do something else.

Trading Toys

Area: Social Skills

Developmental Objectives

- to promote the ability to trade toys
- to promote the development of social skills

Instructions

- Sit on the floor with two or more toddlers as they play with toys. Pick up a toy and play with it for a few minutes. Then say to one of the toddlers, "Would you like to trade toys?" Repeat the word "Trade?" as you hold out your toy to the child. Then model for the child how to exchange your toy for hers. Say thank you and play with the toy the child gives you. If the child shakes her head or says no, then ask another toddler if he would like to trade toys. Play with the traded toy for a while and then offer it to a different child. Continue to do this, making a game of it as you trade toys. Do this activity often so the toddlers begin to understand the concept of trading and begin to learn a few words to interact and trade with one another.

Extensions/Modifications

- Look for opportunities to help the toddlers practice trading. For example, when playing outside, encourage two toddlers to trade shovels in the sandbox. If a child is not interested, then do not force the issue. Also, model trading with another teacher. For example, offer to trade jobs, such as trading wiping off the tables for putting out the food. Make sure that you verbally say what you are doing so the toddlers learn what to say.

Taking Turns

Area: Social Skills

Developmental Objectives

- to promote the ability to take turns
- to promote the development of social skills

Instructions

- Sit on the floor with two toddlers and play with a shape box and shapes. Model taking turns by saying, "It is my turn," and then picking up a block shape and putting it in the shape box. Then say, "Joanna, it is your turn. Choose a block to put in the box." Wait for the child to pick up a block and to find the space in the shape box where it goes. Scaffold the experience by giving clues to toddlers who need help finding the place for their block. For example, say, "You have a square block. Let's find a hole that looks square, like your block." Continue taking turns with the two toddlers, calling each by name, describing what is happening, and saying "It is your turn" as you play.

Extensions/Modifications

- Watch for opportunities throughout the day when you can model and encourage turn-taking. For example, as toddlers play outside, model how to take turns on the riding and climbing toys. Model turn-taking during daily routines as well. For example, say, "Kevin, it is your turn to have your diaper changed. Maddie, your turn will be after Kevin."

Learning to Relate to and Interact with the Environment

Fingerpainting

Area: Classroom Community

Developmental Objectives

- to provide new experiences and interaction with new materials
- to promote participation within the classroom community

Instructions

- Collect old adult-size button-front shirts or T-shirts to use as paint smocks. Set up fingerpaint stations on a low table where the toddlers can stand and easily reach the top. It is a good idea to set this up near a sink where the toddlers can wash their hands afterward.
- Put shaving cream on two trays for two toddlers to fingerpaint. Make a tray for yourself and kneel or sit in a low chair by the children.
- Show the toddlers how to poke at the shaving cream with their fingers and smear it around on the tray. Talk about how the "paint" feels, what the paint smells like, how their hands and fingers look, and the designs that were made with the shaving-cream paint, such as circles and swirls.
- Monitor the toddlers so they do not get the shaving cream in their eyes or put it in their mouths.
- Note that some children may be reluctant to put their hands into the shaving-cream paint. Also, be aware some children are allergic to fragrance, and some have skin allergy reactions to certain types of soaps. Check with families prior to activities that involve materials that could potentially cause allergic reactions.

Extensions/Modifications

- Do not use food as art materials. Food is not something to play with, and it should not be used for art or other activities when it will not be eaten. See other activities that focus on toddlers helping make food to eat, such as Preparing Food in the Classroom on page 111.

Painting Outdoors

Area: Classroom Community

Developmental Objectives

- to promote the ability to play near others
- to promote feelings of connectedness through common play

Instructions

- After the toddlers have had some experience fingerpainting with shaving cream, set up an outdoor painting area. On a warm day, when the toddlers are playing outside, tape very large pieces of fingerpainting paper, butcher's paper, or waxed paper to a low table. Use fingerpaints that are safe for toddlers. Use old adult shirts as painting smocks. Before starting this activity, have all materials ready, including a plan for how the toddlers will wash their hands when they finish painting.
- Encourage two toddlers at a time to move the paint around on the paper with their fingers and hands. Encourage each toddler in the group to paint on the paper. Hang the fingerpaintings to dry.
- When they're dry, hang the class fingerpaintings in the room where the toddlers can see them. Talk with the children about what they did and how they all worked on it, along with the colors, shapes, and textures of the paintings.

Extensions/Modifications

- Teach the toddlers how to put on and take off the painting smocks and how to wash and dry their hands. These self-help skills address toddlers' need for autonomy, boosting their self-confidence and promoting a positive sense of self.

Outdoor Painting Wall

Area: Classroom Community

Developmental Objectives

- to promote participation in a communal play experience
- to promote feelings of connectedness to the classroom community

Instructions

- Set up an area outside for toddlers to paint together. Have shirt smocks for the toddlers to wear. Tape a large piece of paper (several feet long and wide) on an outside wall of the building inside the play area. Set the painting wall up in an area where dripped paint that falls on the ground will not be a problem. Use safe tempera or watercolors for the toddlers to paint the paper with brushes.

- Encourage the toddlers to stand near one another as they paint and talk with them as they do so. Call each child by name. Talk about the colors and marks they make on

the paper. Avoid using praise and instead use encouragement, such as, "You did it. You made a blue line on the painting" or "You are smiling. You feel proud of your painting."

- Write each child's name on the painting and display it at the toddlers' eye level inside the room after the paint dries.

Extensions/Modifications

- Instead of brushes, give the toddlers sponges as their painting tools.
- Cut open large brown-paper bags and cut away the bottom section and handles if there are any. Turn the logo side to the wall and let toddlers paint on the inside. Different types of paper provide opportunities to experience colors and textures and find out how the paint looks different when it's

applied to colored paper versus white paper and slick versus absorbent paper.

- Collect several large appliance-size boxes. Cut a door in one side and windows on the other three sides. Turn the open side of the box down on the playground so the toddlers can paint the outside with tempera paint. When the paint dries, the toddlers can use it as an indoor or outdoor playhouse.

Cleaning the Table

Area: Classroom Community

Developmental Objectives

- to promote participation in classroom activities
- to promote feelings of connectedness to the classroom environment

Instructions

- Fill clean spray bottles with water. Cut up an old T-shirt into pieces.
- Clear a low table and show the toddlers how to spray the table with their water bottles and wipe it off with a cloth.

- Encourage two or more toddlers to clean the table together. Use description to model how to be close and work together to clean the table.

Extensions/Modifications

- Take photographs of the toddlers as they clean the tables. Print and laminate the photographs and put them on a low bulletin

board or wall. Talk with the children about what they did, in the sequence it occurred. This helps toddlers to begin to think about what happens in the order that events occur. Say, "First you sprayed the table. Next you wiped off the table."

- Do the same with other daily routines in the classroom. Change the exhibit of photographs periodically to provide interest and to show new things that the toddlers are able to do for themselves.

Washing Dishes

Area: Classroom Community

Developmental Objectives

- to promote feelings of competence
- to promote feelings of connectedness to the classroom community

Instructions

- On a warm day when toddlers are going to play outside (and not get cold if they get a little wet), put a small amount of warm water in two or more plastic dishpans and set them on a low table in the play yard. Put small, clean yogurt containers and other clean plastic items and toy dishes on the table near the dishpans. Have sponges for washing and pieces of old towels or T-shirts for drying on the table.

- Model for the toddlers how to wash and dry the dishes.
- Remember that health and safety are important criteria for selecting and using toys and all play materials. Be constantly watchful for broken or damaged toys or materials, including sharp edges, splinters, chipping paint, loose nails or screws, and other potential hazards. Do not use large buckets or deep containers of water that toddlers might fall into.

Extensions/Modifications

- Set up a doll bathing table outdoors for toddlers to wash the dolls. Set up a clothes-washing area with a drying rack and let the toddlers wash the dolls' clothes and hang them to dry.

Putting Toys Away

Area: Classroom Community

Developmental Objectives

- to promote participation in common classroom activities
- to promote feelings of connectedness to the classroom community

Instructions

- Take, print, and laminate pictures of toys and other play items. Put the photos on low shelves and bins where the toys are kept.
- Encourage the toddlers to put toys away on the low shelves and in bins where the pictures of the toys are taped.

- At cleanup time, make up a song about putting things away. Sing the song and model how to pick up toys and where to put them. Model cooperation and helping behaviors for toddlers to imitate.

Extensions/Modifications

- Include more than one of the favorite toys so several toddlers can play with the same thing at the same time. However, note that having too many toys and play materials is distracting for toddlers (and also makes cleaning up more difficult).

- Store and rotate toys so the toddlers have enough but not too much. Bringing out toys that have been stored for a few weeks is like having new toys. Toddlers' motor skills are typically developing quickly, and they will be able to do new things with old toys that they previously may not have been able to do.

Making a Playhouse

Area: Classroom Community

Developmental Objectives

- to promote participation in a group classroom project
- to promote feelings of competence
- to promote feelings of connectedness to the classroom community

Instructions

- Collect some large cardboard boxes from an appliance or electronics store. Remove any sharp staples or pieces of metal. Cut windows and doors in the boxes to make several playhouses.
- Encourage the toddlers to go in and out of the box houses. Pretend that one toddler lives there and another comes to visit.

- Call each toddler by name and engage them in visiting one another in their box houses. Pretend and model how to knock on the door and how to ask, "May I come in?" Model other social interaction phrases, such as, "I had a nice visit with you" or "Thank you for letting me visit your house."
- Learn greetings and other words in a toddler's home language. Model these for the toddlers.

Extensions/Modifications

- Pull off two- or three-inch pieces of masking tape in different colors and stick them on a plastic tray near the box house. Show the toddlers how to pull the pieces of tape off the tray and stick them onto the box houses, pretending to put siding or bricks on the houses. Monitor to make sure the children do not put pieces of tape in their mouths.

- Encourage two or more toddlers to work on a box house together. Call each child by name and describe how each is working together to cover the box house.
- Use descriptive words and action words as the toddlers play. Name the colors of tape as the toddlers stick them to the box house.
- Learn descriptive words in a toddler's home language and use these words as he plays in the box house.

Playing Ball

Area: Classroom Community

Developmental Objectives

- to promote the development of motor skills
- to promote participation in classroom community play experiences

Instructions

- Collect several different-size balls and a box or basket low enough for the toddlers to reach into. Show a toddler how to throw a ball into the box or basket. Encourage her to take the ball out and then throw it back into the basket several times. Verbally describe what she is doing. Use descriptive words and action words such as *throw, roll, kick, in,* *out, over, big ball, little ball, red ball,* and so on.

- Turn the basket over on its side and show the toddler how to roll the ball into the basket using her arms and hands. Encourage her to take the ball out and to roll it in again.
- Take the basket outside on the play yard and set it on its side. Show the toddlers how to roll or kick the ball into the basket.

Extensions/Modifications

- Set up two boxes or baskets a few feet apart and encourage two toddlers to play with the balls as described above. Call each toddler by name and talk to both of them about what they are doing, using descriptive words and action words.

- Show the toddlers how to sort the balls by size or color into the baskets. Name the size and color as they play with the balls and sort them. Count the balls in each basket.

Singing and Making Music

Area: Classroom Community

Developmental Objectives

- to promote singing and awareness of music
- to promote participation and interaction within the classroom community

Instructions

- Provide objects that can be used as music makers, such as squeak toys, bells, shaker toys, small empty containers or boxes for drumming, or metal juice can lids inside an empty oatmeal box.
- Model how to make music with the objects. Sing and make music with two or more toddlers.
- Encourage the toddlers to experiment with different objects to make different types of music. Describe the sounds and how they are different.

- Model rhythms and encourage the toddlers to repeat the rhythm pattern. For example, drum on the end of an oatmeal box three times and then pause to encourage the toddlers to repeat the pattern of three. Count "One, two, three" aloud as you drum. Change up patterns and rhythms over time, getting more advanced as the toddlers learn how to do it.

Extensions/Modifications

- Record or videotape the toddlers making music, and then play it back for them to hear or see. Give the toddlers ribbons or scarves to hold and wave as they move to the rhythm of the music.

Going for a Ride on the Bus

Area: Classroom Community

Developmental Objectives

- to promote interaction and participation with others
- to promote feelings of connectedness to the classroom community

Instructions

- Line up two or three toddler-size chairs, one behind the other. Pretend that you are going on a car, bus, or train ride. Put dolls or stuffed animals in some of the chairs and pretend to put a seat belt on the toys. Make motor noises and pretend the bus is getting ready to go. Encourage the toddlers to sit in the chairs and go with you. Call the children by name and pretend to help them put on their seat belts or harnesses. Ask the children on the "bus" if they are ready to go.

- When other toddlers see what you are doing and want to join, add more chairs. Include all the children who want to play,

alternating turns if necessary. Model for the toddlers who are watching to pretend to be people standing on the street and waving to those inside the bus—for example, saying, "Hello, Juan. I see you on the bus," and waving.

Extensions/Modifications

- Pretend you are going somewhere, such as the grocery store. Talk to the children about what they are going to get at the store, repeating and extending, modeling next steps in language development.

- Play this game outside and change where you are going. Maybe you are going to the park, and when you get there, all of the toddlers get off the bus and play. Talk about what you see along the way: "I see white, fluffy clouds" or "I see a brown bird on the fence."

Preparing Food in the Classroom

Area: Classroom Community

Developmental Objectives

- to provide experiences with food in the classroom community
- to promote the development of self-help skills

Instructions

- Provide increased opportunities for the toddlers to help with food preparation, serving themselves, and cleaning up after meals and snacks. Toddlers begin to have food preferences and like to touch and explore the texture and temperature of different types of food. They also like to feed themselves and drink from cups.
- Set up a snack table where the toddlers can take turns helping prepare food, serve themselves, and clean up after snack. Sit at the table and assist the children to cut

up pieces of bananas with a plastic utensil and pour yogurt into a bowl. Other simple snacks could be used to provide the toddlers with opportunities to try new foods and to practice self-help skills.

- Provide snacks and meals that include the types of food eaten in the children's home. Work with staff to plan menus and food choices that are familiar to the toddlers. Sit with the toddlers family style when they eat. Model table manners, social interactions, and how to self-serve food.

Extensions/Modifications

- Being weaned from the bottle is a stressful time for some toddlers. Weaning should be a gradual process, especially in situations where the bottle is used as a security or comfort object. Help such toddlers find a replacement comfort object to use as they are being weaned from the bottle.
- Toddlers may also use meals as a time to exert their growing independence and autonomy. They may say no to certain foods, even the foods they like. Caregivers should not give a lot of attention to food refusals. Otherwise, this behavior may increase and become a way to gain attention from caregivers. Ask, "Do you want green beans or carrots?" and let toddlers choose between the options that are available.
- The size of servings for toddlers should be small. Never force toddlers to eat all of their food or certain types of food. They may occasionally go on food jags where they want the same thing or only a few types of food. Continue to offer different types of food but also have some of the toddlers' favorites available. Respect toddlers' signals that they are full and model words for expressing that they are finished eating. Do not create power struggles over food. Toddlers usually eat when they are hungry. If you have concerns, talk with the child's family.

Looking at Pictures from around the World

Area: Broader Community and Society

Developmental Objectives

- to provide visual experiences of new landscapes, maps, art, and sculptures
- to promote awareness of the broader community, society, and world

Instructions

- Collect posters, brochures, flyers, and other visitor information from local museums, art galleries, and historical societies. These might be included in travel brochures provided by the local chamber of commerce or travel bureau. You can also find photographs online to print. Old magazines such as *National Geographic* and the *Smithsonian* have nice photographs of places from around the world; look for them at thrift stores. Maps are also interesting and might be included. You may want to choose a theme, such as trees, birds, water, people, animals, snow, rain, or clouds to focus and organize this project.
- Laminate the materials to make posters. Display the posters on a wall at toddlers' eye level.
- Notice when the toddlers are looking at the posters. Talk with one or more children about what they are seeing. Point to specific parts of the posters and describe the characteristics of the objects.

- Rotate the posters so the toddlers have new things to look at and talk about.

- Respond to the toddlers' interest and create posters on themes that emerge from their curiosity.

Extensions/Modifications

- Collect brochures, visitor information, programs, and event or exhibit announcements from local museums, art galleries, and historical societies. Display these in an area where families can see them and encourage their participation. Attend these events yourself.

Looking at Art

Area: Broader Community and Society

Developmental Objectives

- to provide opportunities to experience art, culture, and history
- to promote feelings of connectedness to the broader community

Instructions

- Collect photographs of works of art, sculptures, historical monuments, parks, or wildlife areas. Those works of art exhibited in local museums and local monuments, parks, and other sites may be of special interest since families and children may be able to visit them in person.

- Label the photographs in the children's home languages and in English and laminate them. Put holes in the side and attach them with rings or securely tied string to make picture books.
- Sit with a toddler and look at the picture books. Point at the photographs and talk about the paintings, sculptures, landscapes, and objects.

Extensions/Modifications

- Put the picture books where the toddlers can reach them. Create different picture books and rotate them in the play area.
- Make a display using the laminated photographs for families. Inquire about free admission or free days at museums, art galleries, parks, and other sites and post this information for families.
- Invite a speaker from one of the museums or perhaps a park ranger to give a short presentation during a family meeting to help families learn about places to visit and explore.

Looking at Art

Area: Broader Community and Society

Developmental Objectives

- to provide opportunities to experience art, culture, and history
- to promote feelings of connectedness to the broader community

Instructions

- Collect photographs of people working in the types of occupations that are representative of your community and the children's families. If possible, take photographs of people who work in your school building and those who work in the surrounding area. You can include photographs of workers that children might see when they go to the doctor, grocery store, library, and park. Label the photographs in the children's home languages and in English and laminate them. Put holes in the side of the laminated photographs and attach them with rings or securely tied string to make picture books.
- Sit with a toddler and look at the picture books. Point at the photographs and talk about the people, what they are doing, and where the child might see each person.

Extensions/Modifications

- Put the books where toddlers can explore them. Create picture books of local buildings and different workers in your community such as firefighters, police officers, and other community workers. Put toy trucks, cars, and people in the play area that are like the ones in the photographs. Model and encourage imaginative play with the toys.

CHAPTER 8

Social Studies for Toddlers 18 to 24 Months

Understanding and positively responding to toddlers' desires to learn how to use their bodies and their minds helps children develop a sense of autonomy, self-governance, self-control, and self-worth. Toddlers' growing motor and cognitive abilities motivate them to learn and practice new skills and to become independent and capable of doing things for themselves. Creating safe, supportive environments that provide opportunities for toddlers to practice motor skills and to do things by themselves allows them to learn how to make choices and decisions and fosters feelings of confidence and capability. Toddlers then develop a positive sense of self, independence, and autonomy.

Toddlers like to practice taking their shoes, socks, and clothes off and putting them on. They like to make choices about which toys they play with, their play activities, what they eat, and what they do, when. Environments that allow children to make safe, acceptable choices provide opportunities for them to practice decision making, which enhances the development of a capable sense of self. Doing things for themselves helps toddlers develop practical self-help skills, refine their fine- and gross-motor skills, and grow their abilities to self-regulate their emotions and behaviors. Gross-motor skills are those that use large muscles—moving the arms and legs for walking. At this age, toddlers are better able to control their arm movements, and their walking becomes smoother and more coordinated. Fine-motor skills involve the use of more intricate movements, such as finger dexterity—the ability to use a spoon, unzip a jacket, or stack blocks. Power struggles can often be avoided when teachers recognize toddlers' developmental needs to practice new skills and to make decisions as they strive to become more independent and autonomous.

At eighteen months, children are still toddlers. They toddle when they begin to walk, but that quickly changes. Their walking becomes smoother, and they learn to run and jump. They learn to walk up stairs and to ride tricycles and other riding toys. They can throw a ball overhand and kick it forward. Children this age often like to throw objects into the trash can and may put their toys and other things in the trash. Toddlers can take off their clothes with help, and by two years of age, they may be able to put some clothes on by themselves. They can scribble well and are able to stack a tower of two to four blocks. Children in this age group begin to engage in more imaginative play. They like to play with dolls and may begin to pretend to feed them. They also feed themselves and can use spoons and forks. Toddlers at this age can wash and dry their hands and brush their teeth with adult help. Approximately half of their speech is understandable, and they know the names of things and people and can point to pictures of named people and objects. Some toddlers begin to show signs when they need to use the toilet.

From twenty to twenty-two months, toddlers are learning new words every day, and they speak in short, two-word sentences to communicate. They like pretend play and enjoy searching for hidden objects or playing hide-and-seek. Most toddlers explore their bodies—including their genitals—and can identify several body parts. They begin to understand simple opposites like hot and cold. They scribble and can draw lines. They enjoy helping adults do things and imitate other people's behaviors. Listening to music, dancing, and singing are popular activities among this age group.

Toddlers begin to talk about themselves and tell you what they like and do not like. By twenty-three to twenty-four months, toddlers know approximately fifty words. They begin to ask "Why?" or "What's that?" and communicate using two- to three-word sentences. Toddlers like to point at and look at the pictures in books. Toddlers can name five or six body parts on a doll. They notice gender differences and know whether they are a boy or a girl. They like to be around other children and play with them. Toddlers like to sort and arrange objects into categories, along with stacking cubes or blocks. At twenty-four months, toddlers can jump and walk down stairs.

For the following activities, make a copy of the Infant-Toddler Social Studies Activity Observation (see appendix H on the Web Components tab at www .redleafpress.org/itss) for each toddler. Use the form to record how a toddler responds to the activity. Describe how the toddler's verbalizations, facial expressions, and body movements change as he develops. Remember that infants and toddlers with developmental delays, disabilities, or other special needs may need individualized adaptations for these activities. Adaptations should be designed and approved by a child's therapists. See page 30 for additional information.

Learning about Oneself

Looking at Photographs of Children

Area: Sense of Self

Developmental Objectives

- to promote social awareness
- to promote awareness of emotions
- to promote the development of a positive sense of self

Instructions

- Collect photographs from magazines and other print materials that show children's faces. Look for photographs of children that are of different races and ethnicities and from a variety of cultures that are representative of the toddlers in the classroom. Find photographs that show children displaying emotions. Laminate the pictures onto sturdy cardboard, punch holes in the side, and attach with rings or string.

- Sit on the floor with a toddler and look at the Children and Feelings Book. Talk about the faces in the pictures and how the children are feeling. Look at the book with two or more toddlers, encouraging them to sit near one another.

- Make a collage of different faces showing a variety of emotions. Put the collage at eye level where toddlers can look at the faces. Talk with the toddlers about how the children in the photographs are feeling.

Extensions/Modifications

- Read picture books that include stories that describe how people feel and how they express their feelings. As you read the books, point to the faces of people in the pictures and talk about the different facial expressions. Explain how they are feeling with words like *sad*, *happy*, *mad*, *sleepy*, and so on.

- Throughout the day, identify and verbally label toddlers' feelings. Use self-talk to describe how you are feeling and parallel talk to describe what a toddler may be experiencing and feeling. Model problem solving by verbally identifying what is happening, including each toddler's perspective of the situation, and then offering potential actions.

- Toddlers need consistent routines and help with controlling their impulses and emotions. They now know their own names and may begin to express their growing sense of self by showing awareness that some things belong to them, saying "mine" and resisting when someone tries to take the toys they are playing with. Recognize this positive advancement in the development of a sense of self by using encouragement and verbal descriptions such as "You know your name" or "Tell Paul that you are playing with the truck right now." To help toddlers as they develop a healthy sense of self, have more than one of their favorite toys in the classroom. Then you can say, "Paul, there is another truck like the one Mary has in sandbox." Toddlers do not yet understand taking turns and sharing. You can teach them how to play with similar toys or trade toys; this leads to turn-taking and sharing. Sharing is a concept that will be learned later as children's abilities to take the perspective of another person develop.

Playing with Dolls Who Look Like Me

Area: Sense of Self

Developmental Objectives

- to promote the development of a positive sense of self
- to promote pretend play
- to promote language development

Instructions

- Collect ethnically diverse dolls (boys and girls) with a variety of hair colors and textures.
- Have brushes, combs, and other hair care items for toddlers to use on the dolls.
- Collect and make available picture books and photographs that show people with different types of hair, hairstyles, hair care products, and grooming tools.
- Talk with the toddlers and describe different hair colors and textures using words like *curly*, *wavy*, *straight*, *thick*, *fine*, and *coarse*. Point out and describe different lengths and styles of hair.

Extensions/Modifications

- Help toddlers learn about their own hair. Take a photograph of each toddler's hair and hairstyle. Write the child's name on her photograph. Laminate the photographs and make a hairstyles picture book for the class. Sit with a toddler and look at the book. Call each child by name as you point to the photographs. Talk about hair color, texture, and styles, using the words above.
- Ask family members to bring photographs of their hairstyles (or ask if you may take photographs). Pictures from magazines can be used if photographs are not available. Write the child's name and her family members' names on the photographs. Laminate the photographs and make a family hairstyles picture book for each toddler. Sit with each toddler and look at her book. Call the child and family members by name as you point to their names and photographs.

Learning about My Body

Area: Sense of Self

Developmental Objectives

- to promote awareness of bodies
- to teach the names of body parts
- to promote the development of a positive sense of self

Instructions

- Use a crayon to trace each toddler's hands onto a large sheet of paper. Count his fingers as you draw. Have crayons of different skin-tone colors available for the toddlers to color their hands if they want. Note that toddlers should not be required to color inside lines. Scribbling all around and on the drawn hands is the focus of this activity. Write the child's name on his hand picture.
- Put the hand pictures on the wall at toddlers' eye level where the toddlers can see and talk about them.

Extensions/Modifications

- Tape a large piece of paper to the top of a low table, inside or outside. Put different flesh-colored tones of paint in plastic containers large enough for toddlers to put both hands in at the same time. Put a painting smock or old shirt on the toddler before he dips his hands into the paint. Show him how to put his hands in the paint and to make prints on the sheet of paper. Let the toddlers do this two at a time. Have a place for them to wash and dry their hands nearby before taking off their paint smock.
- When they're dry, display the handprint paintings at the children's eye level. Point out the different colors, sizes, and types of handprints and talk with the toddlers about them.

Sometimes I Need to Be Alone

Area: Sense of Self

Developmental Objectives

- to promote self-awareness and awareness of emotional needs
- to promote the abilities to self-regulate and calm self

Instructions

- At times throughout the day, toddlers need a space to be alone, calm themselves, or perhaps just have some quiet time away from the hustle and bustle of other children. Create places in the room where an individual child can be alone to sit or lie down when she feels the need to do so.
- Use self-talk to teach the toddlers how to recognize when they are upset or frustrated. Act out what to do and say when you become upset or angry. Say aloud what it is you think a child is feeling, such as being tired or frustrated, and describe what the child can do to help calm herself. Lead her to a place in the classroom where she can sit or lie quietly to look at a book or hold a stuffed animal. Model for the children that it is okay to remove themselves and to calm themselves when they feel they need a break.

- Use a doll or stuffed animal to act out being tried, frustrated, or upset. Say out loud, "Bear, you need a break." Take the bear to a quiet place in the classroom, such as a child-size rocking chair. "You can rest and calm down here. Come back and play when you feel better."
- Toddlers also need outlets for strong emotions. It isn't okay to hit or kick another child. Give toddlers activities that help them work out aggressive feelings: kicking balls outside, pounding on playdough, or digging and building in wet sand. Carrying objects from one side of the playground to the other or running up and down small hills or mounds of dirt helps toddlers work out feelings as well as exercise their motor skills.

Extensions/Modifications

- Be attentive to toddlers' cues that they may be overstimulated, tired, or frustrated. Encourage the toddlers to take a break and to calm themselves. Teach children how to recognize their feelings, and then teach them socially acceptable ways to verbally describe how they feel. Teach them strategies for how to move away from a highly emotional or volatile situation and calm

themselves down. These are skills that will be used throughout their lives.
- After a child calms down after a tantrum or other emotional event, describe in simple terms what happened and how you think she felt. Help the child reflect on her behaviors and feelings in a nonjudgmental manner to help her understand what happened.

The Shape of My Body

Area: Sense of Self

Developmental Objectives

- to promote awareness of bodies
- to promote the development of a positive sense of self

Instructions

- Draw around a toddler's body with a marker as he lies on the floor on top of a large piece of paper. Write the child's name on the paper. Label each of his body parts on the outline, with *head*, *arm*, *hand*, *leg*, and *foot*.
- Provide skin tone and other colors of crayons for him to scribble on his body outline. Place each child's body picture on the wall.
- Talk with each child about the pictures. Point out eyes, noses, mouths, hair, hands, and feet.
- Read books that describe body parts to the children. Have books about bodies on low shelves or tables for the toddlers to look at and explore during playtime.

Extensions/Modifications

- Use a piece of an old white sheet to make a classroom banner of hand- or footprints. Hang the banner from the ceiling or on a wall.
- Put a large piece of brown paper or an old sheet on an outside sidewalk or smooth outdoor surface. Let the children walk through water-soluble paints and then walk on the old sheet.
- Show the toddlers how to draw around their feet and hands with crayons or chalk.

What My Family Eats

Area: Family

Developmental Objectives

- to promote early literacy skills
- to promote connections to family

Instructions

- Encourage families to take photographs of the foods they eat at home, or cut photographs of different kinds of food from magazines or old cookbooks.
- Make simple food picture books by laminating the photographs or magazine pages, punching holes along one side, and attaching the pages with rings or tied string. On each picture, write the name of the food in the child's home language and in English.
- Hold a toddler on your lap or sit by her and look at her family's food book.

Extensions/Modifications

- Place laminated labeled photographs of the types of food the toddlers eat at home low on a wall or bulletin board. Talk with the toddlers about the photographs and name the foods in the children's home languages and in English. Talk about how families eat different types of food.
- Toddlers are usually feeding themselves finger foods and learning to use spoons and forks.

- If at all possible, provide the children the same types of food they are eating at home. Food should be age appropriate, safe, and nutritious.
- Make snacktime and mealtime social learning times. Toddlers should sit together at a low table with their teacher. Talk with the children about the food, how it looks, how it smells, and how it tastes. Model table manners and using social phrases such as "excuse me," "thank you," "please," "I would like some more bread," or "I am finished eating."

Making Family Snacks

Area: Family

Developmental Objectives

- to promote connections to family
- to promote the development of fine-motor skills

Instructions

- As toddlers gain motor skills and become more coordinated, they enjoy basic cooking activities. Collect recipes of simple foods that children eat at home. Compile the recipes into a cookbook to use in the classroom. Plan cooking experiences such as making instant oatmeal or pudding with chopped fruit, spreading butter or jam on a piece of bread or a cracker, or rolling up a spoonful of beans, rice, and shredded cheese in a tortilla.
- Have all materials ready before beginning this activity with the children and have the toddlers wash and dry their hands before beginning. Sit at a low table with two toddlers at a time as they spread jam on a slice of bread and cut it in half. Use plastic spoons and plastic knives that are not sharp. Sit near, model, and observe as the toddlers make their snack, describing what they do with action words. Talk about the smells, colors, and feel of the jam and bread. After a toddler finishes making and eating her snack, she can wash and dry her hands.
- Take turns so each toddler gets an opportunity to do this.

Extensions/Modifications

- Offer opportunities for the toddlers to peel oranges and slice cucumbers, segments of cantaloupe, mango, papaya, kiwi, and other semisoft vegetables and fruits for snacks.
- Toddlers can pour, mix, and stir ingredients for fruit salads, green salads, or plain instant oatmeal (no sugar or salt added) and spread toppings onto whole-grain baked goods for classroom cooking experiences.

Families

Area: Family

Developmental Objectives

- to promote connections to families
- to promote the development of a positive sense of self

Instructions

- Collect photographs from magazines or online that are of many different families and people—including same-sex parents, grandparents raising grandchildren, mixed-race families, and families from cultures that reflect those of the children in the classroom. Include people with disabilities, young people, old people, and children.

- Laminate the photographs. Make a collage or picture wall at the toddlers' eye level. Talk with the toddlers about things families do together, who the family members are, where they live, what they eat, and how they play.
- Talk with toddlers about how people look different and about their skin colors, hair, eye shapes and colors, facial features, and other characteristics.

Extensions/Modifications

- Create picture books from the photographs for the toddlers to explore. Sit with the toddlers and look at the books.

Learning to Relate to and Interact with Other People

What, Where, How, and When

Area: Communication

Developmental Objectives

- to promote language development
- to promote social development

Instructions

- Play a "What, Where, and When" game with the toddlers. Collect common objects that are safe for children to handle, such as cooking items, household objects, tools, or lawn equipment. As an alternative, find pictures of objects and make sturdy picture books for this activity.
- Sit with one or more toddlers and look at the objects. Pick up an item, such as a spoon, and ask, "What's this?" Pause and wait for the child to say what it is. If he doesn't say what it is, then you say, "This is a big spoon." Next ask, "Where do you use this?" Wait for the toddler to respond and say "kitchen" if he doesn't. Then ask, "When do you use it?" and wait for the toddler to respond. If he doesn't know, say, "We use it to stir things," demonstrating how to stir with the spoon. Use only a few props at first and add more as the children learn what they are.

Extensions/Modifications

- Collect cultural items used in the children's homes and use them as props for the game. Learn the names of the objects in the child's home language and use those names, alternating with English, when you play the game.
- Collect picture books that show common tools such as hammers, screwdrivers, saws, nails, and pieces of wood. Or, make your own books by cutting pictures from magazines, laminating them, and putting them together. Sit with one or more toddlers and play the game, asking what the object is, where you might find it, and when you use it.

Cultural Nursery Rhymes

Area: Communication

Developmental Objectives

- to promote language development
- to promote early literacy skills

Instructions

- Ask families to share nursery rhymes from their home cultures. Collect large nursery rhyme picture books or find large pictures that illustrate a variety of nursery rhymes. Sit with one or more toddlers and read or say two or three nursery rhymes, showing them the book illustrations or pictures. If the nursery rhyme mentions body parts or body movements, act them out. Use gestures and facial expressions.
- As toddlers begin to show preference for certain rhymes, say and act these out often during different times of the day—inside, outside, or during daily routines. Toddlers learn through repetition and enjoy hearing favorite rhymes and stories over and over.

Extensions/Modifications

- Play recordings of nursey rhymes and act them out with the toddlers. Invite families to make recordings of themselves saying nursery rhymes in their home languages.

Animal Mural

Area: Communication

Developmental Objectives

- to promote language development
- to promote cognitive development

Instructions

- On a long piece of butcher or parchment paper, glue pictures cut from magazines or catalogs. Use themes to create murals and change them to provide new learning experiences. Themes might include people, families, cities, farms, animals, insects, houses, or cars and trucks. Label the pictures in block print on the mural. Laminate or cover the paper with clear contact paper. Attach the mural to the wall at toddlers' eye level. Look at the mural with two or more toddlers. Point to pictures and name and describe them. Ask the toddlers to point at pictures as you talk. Say, "I see a brown bear. Where is it?"

Extensions/Modifications

- Collect picture books on the mural themes, sit with two or more toddlers, and read the books. Put toys that reflect the mural theme in the block area or in the outdoor sandbox for toddler play. Model and encourage toddlers' pretend play with the toys.

Looking at Feelings Books

Area: Communication

Developmental Objectives

- to promote language development
- to promote social development

Instructions

- Collect books about friendship, such as *Being Friends* by Karen Beaumont and *My Friend Rabbit* by Eric Rohmann. Also collect books about feelings, such as *Grumpy Bird* by Jeremy Tankard, *Lots of Feelings* by Shelley Rotner, *Baby Faces* by Margaret Miller, and *I Am Happy: A Touch-and-Feel Book of Feelings* by Steve Light. Sit with two toddlers and read the books. Point to pictures, talk with the toddlers about friendship and feelings, and teach them words to communicate with others. Observe for opportunities through the day to use friendship and feelings words to describe and respond to classroom events and experiences.

Extensions/Modifications

- Select books that specifically focus on strong feelings and behaviors that children may be experiencing. Read these books to toddlers and talk with them about the stories and people. For example, to help children cope with anger, include books such as *Mouse Was Mad* by Linda Urban, *Hands Are Not for Hitting* by Martine Agassi, *No Matter What* by Debi Gliori, and *When I Feel Angry* by Cornelia Maude Spelman. Be attentive to the toddlers' fears and experiences and find books that will help them cope. If a toddler is afraid of thunderstorms, read *The Storm Book* by Charlotte Zolotow; if he needs help learning self-control, read *Quiet Loud* by Leslie Patricelli. Include books about grief and death, divorce, and other topics to help children who are experiencing those events to cope and to learn how to communicate their feelings.

Talking to Others about My Clothes

Area: Social Skills

Developmental Objectives

- to promote social development
- to promote language development

Instructions

- As you are getting ready to go outside or when you are sitting with two or more toddlers, call the children by name and talk with them about the clothes they are each wearing and what you are wearing.
- Talk about colors and textures as you touch your own jacket or shirtsleeve. Describe how the fabric feels and what it looks like. Describe designs in the fabric too. "I feel little ridges on my corduroy jacket."
- Then say to one toddler, "May I touch your jacket sleeve?" Pause and wait for the toddler to respond. Model for the children how to gently touch another child's coat, jacket, or shirtsleeve and how to feel the fabric.

- Respect each toddler's space and do not touch their sleeves if they are reluctant or do not want you to do so. You can describe fabrics and clothing without touching them.

Extensions/Modifications

- Do the same activity focusing on shoes or hats. Collect different kinds of hats for the toddlers to try on, look at themselves in the mirror, and talk with others about how they look.

Row, Row, Row Your Boat

Area: Social Skills

Developmental Objectives

- to promote social interactions and social development
- to promote pretend play

Instructions

- Help the toddlers interact with one another. Sing "Row, Row, Row Your Boat," encouraging two toddlers to hold hands as they sit on the floor and sway or rock back and forth to the music, pretending to row the boat.
- Call the children by name and describe how they are helping row the boat.

Extensions/Modifications

- Play other simple games such as "Ring around the Rosy" and "London Bridge." Encourage the children to hold hands and to act out the song.
- Say nursery rhymes such as "Jack and Jill," "Humpty Dumpty," and "Hey, Diddle, Diddle," and encourage toddlers to act them out.

Rolling a Ball

Area: Social Skills

Developmental Objectives

- to promote the development of gross- and fine-motor skills
- to promote social development

Instructions

- Collect several balls of different sizes, colors, and weights. Select a ball and sit on the floor a few feet in front of two toddlers. Roll the ball to one of the toddlers, calling her by name. Encourage her to roll it back to you. Then say, "Now it is Jack's turn" and roll the ball to the other child. Describe what you are doing: "I'm rolling the ball to Jack. Roll it back to me."

- Encourage turn-taking and promote interaction as the toddlers learn to play near and with one another. It may be helpful to have two balls, one for each toddler, when you first begin teaching this activity.

Extensions/Modifications

- Alternate pairings of toddlers so that they all have an opportunity to get to know and play near each child in the classroom. Call each child by name as you play with the ball(s). Learn the word *ball* in each child's home language and alternate using it with the English word as you play with the toddlers.

What's in the Box?

Area: Social Skills

Developmental Objectives

- to promote social development
- to promote language development
- to promote cognitive development

Instructions

- Collect safe objects of different types, textures, hardness, and shapes. Things like small stuffed animals, balls, blocks, books, and other common objects that children play with are good ones to use. Get a cardboard box with a lid and cut a hole in one end large enough for a toddler to put her arm through.
- Place an object in the box, sit with two or more toddlers, and show them how to reach in and feel the object.

- Start with one object, and then add another as the toddlers learn what to do. Call each child by name and describe turn-taking as the children play the game.
- Let each toddler take a turn reaching inside and feeling the object. Say, "Kate, it's your turn."
- Say, "What is it?" then pause and wait for the toddler to think about what she is feeling and try to figure out what it is. Ask questions such as "Does it feel soft or

hard?" and "Is it big or little?" and "Is it cold or warm?" Think of other questions to ask, depending on the object you have hidden. If the toddler attempts to name the object or does name the object, elaborate and expand on what she says.

Extensions/Modifications

- Each day, put a new object in the box. Take turns playing the game with each toddler or several at a time, taking turns.

- Leave the box out for the toddlers to play with on their own.

Learning to Relate to and Interact with the Environment

Playing on a Balance Beam

Area: Classroom Community

Developmental Objectives

- to promote the development of gross-motor skills
- to promote feelings of connectedness to the classroom community

Instructions

- Put a heavy board approximately four feet long by one foot wide and one inch thick on the floor (or outside on a smooth surface) for toddlers to walk on and practice balance.
- Show two or more toddlers how to walk on the board without touching the floor or ground.

- Encourage the two toddlers to walk on the board, one behind the other. *Note*: Make sure the board is heavy enough not to flip up at one end when a toddler steps on it.
- Call the children by name and describe what they are doing.

Extensions/Modifications

- Show the toddlers how to step over the board. Encourage two toddlers to step over the board at the same time.
- As the toddlers' motor skills develop, show them how to stand on the board and jump off. Encourage two toddlers to stand side by side and jump off together.

- Make different types of balance beams using piles of newspapers or stacked up magazines. Tape the bundles together in long strips for the toddlers to walk on and over.

Obstacle Course

Area: Classroom Community

Developmental Objectives

- to promote the development of gross-motor skills
- to promote feelings of connectedness to the classroom community

Instructions

- Toddlers like to practice new motor skills. Create an obstacle course for them that includes places to climb in and over, crawl onto and into, step on and over, and jump on. Some items to use include rolled up blankets; a large, clean box with the ends cut out; large, firm pillows; a crib mattress; a board to walk on and over; fabric tents or tunnels; Hula-hoops; and nonslip rugs of different sizes and textures.

- Encourage the toddlers to move through the obstacle course. Stay close and watch to make sure the area does not get too crowded as the toddlers play. Call each child by name and describe what he is doing. Use action words to describe what each child does, such as *climbing*, *walking*, *jumping*, *crawling*, *rolling*, and so on.
- Play follow the leader, with the toddlers taking turns following one another through the obstacle course.

Extensions/Modifications

- Create an outdoor obstacle course using a wide board to walk on, a piece of cloth or rope to jump over, a box with the ends cut out to crawl through, and other safe materials.

Drumming

Area: Classroom Community

Developmental Objectives

- to promote awareness of music
- to promote social development

Instructions

- Use a large plastic storage container or a big empty box as a drum for several toddlers to play at the same time.
- Place the drum on the floor and kneel next to it as you model how to use your hand to pat the top of the drum.
- Pat the drum and encourage one or more toddlers to imitate the pattern of drumming you model.

Extensions/Modifications

- Sing or play music and model for the toddlers how to keep time to the music by patting on the top of the drum. Encourage the toddlers to stand near one another as they play the drum.

Making Applesauce

Area: Classroom Community

Developmental Objectives

- to promote the development of fine-motor skills
- to promote cognitive development
- to promote social development

Instructions

- Make applesauce for the toddlers' snack. At the beginning of the day, peel and cut up an apple for each toddler. Encourage the children to watch as you do this, talking to them about what you are doing and how the apples smell and feel.
- Take turns letting each toddler put her apple pieces into a slow cooker pot. Add a little water, letting a toddler pour it in. Plug in the slow cooker and cook the apples out of reach of the children. Stir occasionally.
- In the afternoon, spoon applesauce into small bowls for the toddlers. Sit at a table with the toddlers while they eat their applesauce. Describe what's happening and use different types of talk with the toddlers about how the food tastes as they practice eating with spoons. See pages 26–27 to review ways of talking to toddlers that promote their learning.

Extensions/Modifications

- Involve the toddlers in making simple snacks and trying new foods. As their motor skills develop, let toddlers serve themselves.
- Introduce fruits and vegetables such as mango, papaya, and kiwi to the toddlers. Let them see the fruit whole; then let them cut up pieces with safe plastic knives and eat the fruit. Talk with the toddlers as they do these things.

Growing Taller

Area: Classroom Community

Developmental Objectives

- to promote the development of a positive sense of self
- to promote social development

Instructions

- Toddlers begin to get taller during this time, and they feel proud of how tall they are and what they can do. Put a large strip of paper on the wall to use as a place to measure each toddler's height, writing the children's names on the measurements. Talk with each toddler about how tall she is.
- After measuring all the children, encourage two or three toddlers to stand together with their backs to their measurements on the paper. Take a photograph of the toddlers by their measurements. Laminate the photograph onto cardboard and write each child's name on the front.
- Make a classroom album of the photographs. Keep the album in an area where the toddlers can look at it during the day.
- Talk with the toddlers and call each child by name as you point to her photograph.

Extensions/Modifications

- Repeat the above activity every three to four months so that children can see how much they have grown. You could also weigh the children on a scale and record their weight on their photograph along with their height measurement.

Flannel Board People

Area: Classroom Community

Developmental Objectives

- to promote imaginative play
- to promote social development

Instructions

- Make a photo doll of each child by taking full-body photographs of each child. Print and cut out the photos. Write the child's name on her photograph and laminate it onto cardboard to make a flannel board person. Glue a piece of felt or put a piece of Velcro on the back of each person's photograph and put them on a flannel board at toddlers' eye level. Make a doll of yourself and other teachers too.

- Show the toddlers how to put the people on the flannel board. Call each doll by the child's name. Count the dolls and sort them into boys and girls, children and adults, or by the colors of their clothing.

- Put the photo dolls in a bin near the flannel board where the toddlers can play with them.

Extensions/Modifications

- Make photo dolls of the children's families. Talk to each toddler about his family, calling each member by name.
- Make a collage of the photographs on a large piece of poster board. Label the collage "People in Our Classroom" and look at it with one or more toddlers, talking about the people in your classroom. Call each person by name.
- Print the photographs on specialized transfer paper that produces an iron-on for cloth. Iron each photograph onto a plain T-shirt and give each child the T-shirt with his photograph on it.

Clothing from Many Cultures

Area: Broader Community and Society

Developmental Objectives

- to learn about different cultures
- to promote feelings of connectedness to the broader community

Instructions

- Collect a variety of different clean hats, scarves, shoes, belts, and items of clothing worn in the children's home cultures. Do not include clothing with small items that might be removed and swallowed. Check any buttons or fasteners to make sure they are safe and secure.

- Make an area where the toddlers can try on and play with the hats and clothing. Talk with the children about different types of clothes.
- Encourage the children to try on hats and clothes and to look at themselves in the mirror.

Extensions/Modifications

- Find photographs in magazines of people around the world wearing traditional hats, clothing, shoes, and cultural objects that are representative of the children's home cultures. Laminate and display the pictures in a collage on the wall at the toddlers' eye level.

My Neighborhood

Area: Broader Community and Society

Developmental Objectives

- to learn about the neighborhood
- to promote feelings of connectedness to the broader community

Instructions

- Take photographs of the neighborhood and community. Include photographs of the grocery store, fire station, post office, school, park, and other prominent places in the community. Ask families to bring photographs of their houses or apartments or perhaps a room inside.

- Label the photographs, laminate them, and bind them together to make a neighborhood book.
- Sit with one or more toddlers and look at the book. Talk about the different places. Point to and name what they are and what people do there.

Extensions/Modifications

- Collect photographs from magazines or newspapers of the type of work that children's families do. Laminate the pictures onto heavy cardboard and label them. Sit

with one or more toddlers and look at the books. Point to the pictures and talk about what the people are doing.

Listening to Music and Singing

Area: Broader Community and Society

Developmental Objectives

- to promote musical skills and awareness
- to promote feelings of connectedness to the broader community

Instructions

- Invite children's families and others from the community to visit the classroom to share music or sing with the toddlers. Make these visits short, approximately five to ten minutes, and informal.

- Give the toddlers musical instruments and sound makers to keep time with the music as they sing.
- Talk with the toddlers as they watch and listen to musical instruments, singing, or perhaps the reading of a children's story or poem in a child's home language.

Extensions/Modifications

- Families may not be able to come during the day. Invite them to play a musical instrument, sing a song, or read a short book for five minutes in the classroom when they drop off or pick up their children.

What's That Music?

Area: Broader Community and Society

Developmental Objectives

- to promote musical skills and awareness
- to promote feelings of connectedness to the broader community

Instructions

- Invite local musicians to play music for the toddlers and to introduce them to different types of music, instruments, and styles of singing. Musicians or singers might set up in a common area of the school where groups of children from different classrooms listen for short periods of time. This setup would give all the children in the school or program an opportunity to participate.
- Talk with the toddlers about what they hear. Name the types of music and instruments.
- Encourage the toddlers to sing along and to keep time with the music.
- Invite families to come and listen.

Extensions/Modifications

- Invite artists and musicians to present at parent meetings. Have discussions on culture, the arts, and music with the families.
- Invite families to videotape themselves singing or playing music at home and share these recordings with you. Play the recordings as you sit with the toddlers and talk with them about what they are hearing or seeing.

People and What They Do

Area: Broader Community and Society

Developmental Objectives

- to promote feelings of connectedness to the broader community
- to promote awareness of people from around the world

Instructions

- Cut photographs from magazines that show people working, cooking, eating, sleeping, playing, swimming, bicycling, and so on. Note that not all people sleep on a bed or eat at a table, so look for pictures that show a variety of lifestyles and living arrangements, as well as races, ethnicities, and cultures.

- Laminate the pictures on heavy cardboard, punch holes in the side of the pages, and put them together with rings or string.

- Sit with a toddler and look at the book with her. Talk about what the person on each page is doing and engage the toddler by asking questions about the pictures.

Extensions/Modifications

- Make books that show common activities in different environments. For example, if you are in a large city, include photographs of people riding on buses or trains. For children in rural farm areas, include pictures of tractors, animals, and people doing farmwork.

- Sit with two or more toddlers and look at a book. Show the children how to look at the book together.

CHAPTER 9

Social Studies for Two-Year-Olds

Two-year-olds can be described as both busy and active. Their growing motor abilities and expanding language capabilities propel them into the world. They are curious and want to know and learn about everything they see. This is also a time for growing independence since they can now do many things for themselves. Two-year-olds strive for autonomy and may say, "Me do it."

They may also talk to themselves, repeating what they have heard adults say. For example, when you show a toddler how to put on a jacket, you describe what you are doing, giving instructions aloud while using body movements to demonstrate for the child. At a later time, she may try to remember how to do this for herself and repeat your instructions aloud to help guide her body movements. Toddlers' talking out loud to themselves eventually transforms into their inner speech and learned behaviors, including social skills and social expectations. This internalization of social rules and expectations is the process by which young children develop the ability to regulate their own behavior and have self-control. Talking with young children about how their behavior affects others, how others feel, and how they themselves feel when things happen to them helps two-year-olds develop an awareness of how their behavior has consequences not only for themselves but also for others.

By twenty-four months of age, toddlers are usually walking well and learning to jump. They can walk down stairs and climb. Two-year-olds can feed themselves using utensils, name their body parts, and make short sentences. They express a wide range of emotions and are beginning to understand some abstract concepts such as now and later. Toddlers this age like to arrange objects into categories and match objects. They are also becoming aware of gender differences and may be able to tell you if they are a boy or a girl. Two-year-olds' fine-motor skills enable them to stack up several blocks to build a tower and to scribble with crayons and draw a vertical line. They like to throw things and can typically throw a ball overhand.

135

For the following activities, make a copy of the Infant-Toddler Social Studies Activity Observation (see appendix H on the Web Components tab at www.redleafpress.org/itss) for each toddler. Use the form to record how a toddler responds to the activity. Describe how the toddler's verbalizations, facial expressions, and body movements change as she develops. Remember that infants and toddlers with developmental delays, disabilities, or other special needs may need individualized adaptations for these activities. Adaptations should be designed and approved by a child's therapists. See page 30 for additional information.

Learning about Oneself

I'm Here Today

Area: Sense of Self

Developmental Objectives

- to promote social development
- to promote the development of a positive sense of self

Instructions

- Take a photograph of each toddler. Laminate the photograph onto cardboard. Write each child's name on a strip of paper and attach Velcro to the back of the paper and to the child's photograph.
- Create an area (such as a bulletin board) near the classroom entrance for the photographs. Greet the toddlers on arrival and give them their name strips to put on their photographs. Say, "I'm glad you are here today."
- After all the toddlers have arrived each morning, talk with them about who isn't at school that day. Tell them why the missing toddler isn't there. Call each toddler by name, point to his photograph, and say whether he is in the classroom.

Extensions/Modifications

- Do the reverse at the end of the day as the children are getting ready to go home. They can take their names down from the bulletin board and put them in a "Going Home" box.

Teachers can tell toddlers good-bye and that they will see them tomorrow. Creating rituals for coming and going helps toddlers make transitions more easily.

My Skin Color

Area: Sense of Self

Developmental Objectives

- to promote social development
- to promote the development of a positive sense of self

Instructions

- Buy several packages of knee-high stockings in different shades. Include black, brown, tan, red, pink, yellow, and white.
- Show the children how to put their hands and arms into the stockings and stretch them over their arms. Use the stockings to talk about how people have different skin colors.

- Ask each child to find a stocking that is like the color of her skin. Ask her to try on different colors.
- Ask questions and talk with the children to help them learn about different skin tones and ethnic backgrounds. Review the different ways to talk with children on pages 26–27.

Extensions/Modifications

- Put the stockings in a plastic bin on a low shelf where the children can play with them.
- Have books available that include people of all skin tones and of all ages available for the toddlers to look at, talk about, and explore.

- Have dolls for children to play with that have different skin tones, eye shapes, and hair textures and colors.

Playing with Dough

Area: Sense of Self

Developmental Objectives

- to promote the development of fine-motor skills
- to promote the use of play and physical activity to express feelings

Instructions

- Poking and pounding dough and clay are good ways for toddlers to express and deal with strong feelings such as anger and frustration. These activities are also sensory experiences that help build fine-motor skills.

- Cover a low table with a protective sheet (or use individual trays) for working with the dough or clay. Show the toddlers how to poke, pound, roll balls, and make ropes with the dough. Have small, sturdy plastic hammers for pounding and objects for poking holes in the dough. Provide blunt scissors for cutting ropes of dough. Monitor the toddlers' use of the scissors and stay nearby to help.

Extensions/Modifications

- Use skin-toned clay or dough that air dries and hardens. Show the toddlers how to flatten the clay into circles using rolling pins. Model for the children how to make a handprint by pressing their hands onto to the clay. Poke a hole in the top of the clay mold with a pencil or straw. Use a tooth-pick to write the toddlers' names on their handprints. Let the clay dry and then let the toddlers push a piece of ribbon or string through the hole for hanging. If flesh-toned clay is unavailable in some of the children's skin tones, have all the toddlers use skin-toned washable paints to color their handprints. Hang the hands around the room.
- When a toddler is feeling angry, say, "You are mad. You can pound on the playdough to help get those mad feelings out." Or help direct the child to another physical outlet for her strong feelings: "You can ride the tricycle and help get out those feelings," or "Kick the ball toward the fence to help you get out those mad feelings."

Quiet Place

Area: Sense of Self

Developmental Objectives

- to promote emotional development
- to promote the development of a positive sense of self
- to promote the ability to self-regulate

Instructions

- Create a quiet place for the toddlers to retreat to when they need time to calm themselves or to be away from the action of a busy classroom. A large plastic bin with low sides that a toddler can climb into or a large box turned on its side work well. Hang a soft, sheer piece of fabric over the plas-tic bin to create a see-through tent. Cover the inside of the space with a soft blanket or rug. Include a couple of pillows, stuffed animals, and a book or two. Toddlers may want to select a special stuffed toy or book to take with them to the quiet place.
- Introduce the quiet place as an area where a child decides for himself when he wants to go there. For example, say, "Sometimes I get upset and can't think. Everyone feels like this sometimes. I go to a quiet place to calm down. When I feel better and I am ready to be with other people, then I come out of the quiet place."

You can act this out for the child, pretending to be sad, mad, or upset in some way. Go to the quiet place and hold a stuffed animal or look at a book for a few seconds. Then say, "I feel better. I calmed myself and I'm ready to play again."

You should be able to see the child at all times, including when he is in the quiet place. The quiet place should never be used as punishment. The idea is for toddlers to begin to recognize their feelings and personal needs to calm themselves, to regain self-control, and to monitor their own behavior.

Extensions/Modifications

When children are playing outside, they may also need a place to go to where they can calm themselves. A large, clean plastic barrel that has been turned on its side and stabilized with boards or stones laid beside it on the ground to keep it from rolling is one idea. Put a soft indoor-outdoor rug inside of the barrel. In preparing the outdoor quiet place, you might have the toddlers paint or decorate the outside of the barrel as an outdoor project.

My Favorites

Area: Sense of Self

Developmental Objectives

- to promote social development
- to promote cognitive development
- to promote the development of a positive sense of self

Instructions

- Take two or three photographs of each toddler doing things in the classroom or outdoors, such as playing with a favorite toy, looking at her favorite book, or eating her favorite food. Laminate the photographs onto heavy cardboard to make picture cards. On the back of each card, write the child's name and her favorite toy, book, or food.
- Sit on the floor with two or three toddlers. Put their picture cards in a small basket or bin and shuffle them around. Play a matching game by asking a toddler to draw a card out of the container and then match it to the person pictured.
- Talk about who is in the picture, calling the child by name, and talk about her favorite thing. Point out how the toddlers have different toys, books, and food in their photographs. Describe how people are different and like different things. Talk about how wonderful and interesting it is that people are different and like different things.

Extensions/Modifications

- Rotate the photographs and play the game with different toddlers. Take new photographs as the toddlers' preferences change as they grow and develop.

- Place the container of photographs on a low shelf or table where toddlers can play with the picture cards. Teach them how to play a matching game by finding all the photographs of one child and placing them together.

Names for Feelings

Area: Sense of Self

Developmental Objectives

- to promote emotional development
- to promote social development
- to promote language development

Instructions

- Sit with one or more toddlers on the floor and sing a feelings song such as "When You're Happy and You Know It."
- Sing the song using other feeling words such as *sad*, *angry*, *tired*, and *scared*.

- Use different body movements to illustrate each of the feelings, such as *clap your hands*, *stomp your feet*, and *take a nap*.

Extensions/Modifications

- Read a story to one or more toddlers about feelings. For example, *Alexander and the Terrible, Horrible, No Good, Very Bad Day* by Judith Viorst shows facial expressions of a child experiencing different feelings. For toddlers, whose attention span may not be long enough for the entire book, look at and point to the pictures of the child's face. Talk about how the child in the story is feeling.

- Teach words for feelings and provide examples of ways that toddlers can express feelings and get their needs met. Ask questions such as "Why do you think he is sad?" There are no wrong answers, and the toddlers' responses do not have to be related to the written story. Use books in creative ways that allow toddlers to bring their own meanings to the pictures.

My Individual Needs

Area: Sense of Self

Developmental Objectives

- to promote emotional development
- to promote the development of a positive sense of self
- to promote the ability to self-regulate

Instructions

- Open communication and a trustful relationship between families and caregivers help support toddlers' development and well-being. Observe toddlers, talk with families, and be aware of toddlers' current interests and experiences. Collect and read books to individuals and small groups of toddlers that focus on topics that relate to their emotional needs, current experiences, and family events. For example, if a toddler has a new baby sibling, has moved to a new house, or has been to the doctor, add and read books that help the toddler process these events.
- Seeing how others react and respond to similar events helps young children learn coping strategies and understand that other people have experiences and feelings that are similar to their own.

Extensions/Modifications

- Collect books with longer stories and read them to two or more toddlers at a time. Toddlers learn through repetition, so select books that have rhymes and repeating phrases. Read the same books to the toddlers over and over, encouraging them to repeat and read along as they learn the words.
- Rotate books in the areas where children select and look at books by themselves. Make books of shapes, animals, and people. Laminate old greeting cards, photographs, or pictures from magazines, punch holes in them, and fasten them together with rings or string.

Playing Dress Up

Area: Family

Developmental Objectives

- to promote connections to family
- to promote the development of a positive sense of self
- to promote social development

Instructions

- Have clothes and props that are like the ones toddlers' families wear at home and at work. Have toddler-size props for the children to imitate adult work and activities. Examples are farmers, doctors, cooks and bakers, firefighters, police, bus drivers, janitors, and train engineers.

- Set up an area in the classroom where the toddlers can reach and put on the clothes and play with the props. Use the ideas for talking with toddlers presented on pages 26–27 as you stay near and talk with them about what they have on and what they are doing.

Extensions/Modifications

- Look at and read picture books to the toddlers about different types of work and workers.

My Family and Pets

Area: Family

Developmental Objectives

- to promote connections to family and pets
- to promote the development of a positive sense of self

Instructions

- Ask families to bring photographs of themselves and their children, their home, pets, and special objects. Create a family photo album for each toddler. Label each family member, pet, and object in the album. For children whose home language is not English, include names and descriptions in both the home language and English.
- Sit with a child and let him go through his album and tell you about his family. Learn the names of objects pictured in the album in the child's home language. Use descriptive words and questions to engage him in talking about himself and his family. Help him feel pride about himself and his family.

- Keep the photograph albums in a container on a low shelf or table where the children can look at them during playtime. Observe the toddlers to see how they describe themselves and their families to other children.

Extensions/Modifications

- Use a photograph of a child and a separate photograph of his family to make a matching game. Laminate or cover each photo with a plastic sleeve. Keep the photographs in a container on a low shelf or table where the children can play with them and match one another to their families.

Snack and Mealtime Placemats

Area: Family

Developmental Objectives

- to promote connections to family
- to promote the development of a positive sense of self
- to promote cognitive development
- to promote the development of fine-motor skills

Instructions

- Take photographs of the children and their families during drop-off and pickup times. Print the photographs and put them in a small plastic bin on a table, along with glue sticks and eleven-by-eighteen-inch sheets of heavy construction paper in different colors.
- Sit at the table with two toddlers as they look through the photographs and find the pictures of themselves and their families. Let the toddlers use a glue stick to paste their photographs onto the construction paper. If this is the toddlers' first experience with glue sticks, model how to use them by making your own placemat.
- Write "My Family," the child's name, and the family members' names on the placemat. See pages 26–27 for different ways to talk with toddlers while they make their placemats to provide a rich learning experience.
- Laminate or cover both sides of the placemats with clear contact paper, sealing the edges to keep them from getting wet. At snacktime and mealtime, let the toddlers put their placemats on the table to use.

Extensions/Modifications

- The toddlers can take their placemats home and make new placemats throughout the year as they grow and develop and as their families change.
- Use themes for the toddlers to make other placemats, such as "My Favorite Foods." Let them cut photographs of food (or whatever the theme) from magazines.

Learning to Use the Toilet

Area: Family

Developmental Objectives

- to promote connections to family
- to promote the development of a positive sense of self
- to promote self-help skills

Instructions

- Have dolls with clothing that the toddlers can practice putting on and taking off. Include doll clothing with zippers, buttons, and snaps. Include doll size diapers and underpants with the dolls. Put the dolls in a dramatic play area along with a doll-size toilet where the toddlers can play with the dolls and pretend that the dolls are using the toilet.

Extensions/Modifications

- Sit with one or more toddlers and read *Diapers are Not Forever* by Elizabeth Verdick to the toddlers. Put the book on a low shelf or table where toddlers can look at it by themselves.
- Have a family meeting to discuss toilet teaching and coordinating the process between home and school. Make a list of developmental behaviors that indicate readiness for toilet learning for families and write a description of how toddlers are taught to use the toilet at school. Provide families with suggestions for what types of clothing are helpful to toddlers as they learn to undress and dress themselves during toileting. It is helpful if families and teachers use the same words for toilet learning. For children whose home languages are not English, learn the words families are using for toileting and use both the home language and English for toilet teaching. For additional information on toilet teaching, visit the Zero to Three website at www.zerotothree.org/resources/266-potty-training-learning-to-the-use-the-toilet.

Learning to Relate to and Interact with Other People

Singing Songs

Area: Communication

Developmental Objectives

- to promote musical skills and awareness
- to promote social development

Instructions

- Sing a song or play music with two or more toddlers. Teach the toddlers simple songs such as "Twinkle, Twinkle Little Star" and "Old MacDonald." As you sing, clap your hands, shake, sit, stand, jump, sway, and move in time to the music. Give the toddlers pieces of ribbon or scarves to wave around as they sing and move. Learn songs and play music from toddlers' home cultures.

Extensions/Modifications

- Take photographs of the toddlers moving and making music and make a collage to display low on a wall where the toddlers can see the pictures and talk about them.

Sailing on the Ocean

Area: Communication

Developmental Objectives

- to promote social development
- to promote language development

Instructions

- Draw or cut out photographs of fish, dolphins, whales, seals, and other ocean creatures. Laminate them on heavy cardboard.
- Fold two blankets and put them on the floor. Put a Hula-hoop on top of each blanket, making a spot for a toddler to sit or lie down inside the "boat." Place the ocean creatures around the pretend boats.
- Play Sailing on the Ocean with two toddlers by encouraging them to sit or lie down on the blankets inside the hoops. Pretend that they are floating on water and describe to them that their boats are bobbing up and down and floating near each other.
- Encourage each toddler to wave to the other and to say hello. Ask them questions such as "Where are you going?" as they pretend to be riding on their boats.
- Use descriptive words to talk about what they see and what they are doing. Also review ways of talking with toddlers on pages 26–27.

Extensions/Modifications

- Use the same idea but with cars and pretend the toddlers are going on a trip. Change the props around the cars to include objects, buildings, and things a child might see on a trip through the desert, mountains, or a city.
- Name the objects and describe them to the children as they are going on their trip. Make sounds that they might hear and encourage them to use their imagination.
- Add additional boats or cars as the toddlers get older and develop the ability to interact with two or more people at a time.

Playing with Puppets

Area: Communication

Developmental Objectives

- to promote social development
- to promote language development
- to promote dramatic play

Instructions

- Collect puppets shaped like animals, birds, sea creatures, insects, and people. Use a large cardboard appliance box to make a puppet theater. Put the puppets into bins based on themes or categories. Model acting out short stories with the puppets and show the toddlers how to put on puppet shows for one another.
- Use descriptive words for the puppets' actions, make animal sounds, and make up dialogue for the puppets to say to one another. Also review ways of talking with toddlers on pages 26–27.

Extensions/Modifications

- Read books to the toddlers about animals and people. Act out the stories with the puppets and encourage the toddlers to do the same. Select books that focus on feelings, social interactions, and problem solving for the children to imitate with the puppets.

A Book about Me

Area: Communication

Developmental Objectives

- to promote social development
- to promote language development
- to promote the development of a positive sense of self

Instructions

- Use card stock to make pages for a book. On the cover, write *A Book about Me*. On the second page, write *My name is* _____. Write the following statements on the subsequent pages: *I am* _____ *years old. I like the color* _____. *I like to eat* _____. *I like to play* _____. Sit with two toddlers and interview them as you write their names and favorite things in their books. Have crayons ready for the toddlers to draw pictures in their books, or supply old magazines for them to cut out pictures to paste in their books. Laminate the pages, punch holes on one side, and attach the pages with yarn. Sit with the toddlers and read their books to them. Use descriptive words to talk about the illustrations that the children have used in their books. Also review ways of talking with toddlers on pages 26–27.

Extensions/Modifications

- Create books based on themes such as My Favorite Foods, My Family, My Favorite Toys, and My Friends. Sit with two or more toddlers and read their books to them. Toddlers can take their books home to share with their families.

Find Our Friends

Area: Social Skills

Developmental Objectives

- to promote cognitive development
- to promote social development

Instructions

- Play a variation of the game hide-and-seek with the toddlers to teach them the names of other children and to emphasize the value of friends and of each child in the classroom. Play the game with two toddlers to begin with and increase the number of children as they get older.
- Tell the children you are going to play Find Our Friends.
- Close your eyes and count to ten while the children hide. When you finish counting, say, "I am looking for my friends. Here I come."
- As you find a child, say, "I found my friend Crystal. Now we are looking for our friend Max. Here we come." Look for the other child.
- When you find him, say, "We found all our friends, Max and Crystal." Play the game again.

Extensions/Modifications

- Play the game outside and hold hands with the children as you find them. Make a chain of people holding hands as you look for other hiding children. When you find everyone, make a circle, say, "We found all of our friends," and name each child.

Simon Says

Area: Social Skills

Developmental Objectives

- to promote cognitive development
- to promote social development

Instructions

- Play Simon Says with two or more toddlers.
- Use the game to teach the toddlers how to sit or play near another child or use gentle touch. For example, say, "Simon says stand near a friend," or "Simon says gently touch a friend's arm."

Extensions/Modifications

- Observe continually for toddlers who may be reluctant to join activities or who need additional support to be near others. Model for the toddlers how to enter play with other children. Say aloud what a child might say and model what to do. For example, if you notice a child watching another child play, say, "You are watching Jasmine build with blocks. You can sit near her and build with blocks close to her."
- More outgoing toddlers may disrupt the play of others in an attempt to be involved. They may knock down block towers built by other children or do other things to try to get the children's attention or to be involved in an activity. Describe what you think the toddler wants to do, such as, "You want to play with Destiny and Katlynn." Say aloud what he might say and model what to do. "Sit here and play." Show the toddler how to sit near others and play with the same types of toys. Stay close and describe for the toddlers what each one is doing.
- Social skills are learned, and it takes time to know how to enter into play and to know what to say to others. Model for toddlers what to do and say. Use self-talk and parallel talk to teach them how to socially interact. Review ways to talk with toddlers on pages 26–27.

Making Footprints Together

Area: Social Skills

Developmental Objectives

- to promote cognitive development
- to promote sensory development
- to promote social development

Instructions

- On a warm day, tape a long piece of brown paper (or use brown grocery bags) on a smooth outdoor surface. Mix up washable tempera paints in several colors and put the paints in containers large enough for a toddler to put both feet inside. Have paint shirts for the toddlers to put on over their clothes.
- Help each toddler put her feet into the paint and then walk on the paper. Make sure that the toddlers are safe and do not slip down as they do this. Take turns with one or two toddlers making footprints on the paper at a time. Talk with the toddlers about colors, how the paint feels, and different sizes of feet. After a toddler finishes walking on the paper, wash her feet with a hose or in a plastic tub of water and dry her feet. Put her shoes back on her before she returns to play on the playground while the other toddlers make footprints.
- Hang the dry footprint paintings on the wall of the classroom for the toddlers to look at and talk about as they play.

Extensions/Modifications

- Hang a long piece of paper or an old sheet on an outdoor wall. Provide the toddlers containers of washable tempera paint, paint rollers, and brushes, and let them paint on the paper or fabric. When it's dry, hang the painting in the classroom or use the fabric to make a banner to hang with a dowel rod.

Making Music

Area: Social Skills

Developmental Objectives

- to promote musical skills and awareness
- to promote the development of gross- and fine-motor skills
- to promote social development

Instructions

- Make small drums and shakers for the toddlers to play with by collecting empty round oatmeal boxes and large plastic yogurt or cottage cheese containers. Put rocks, small jar lids, or other small items inside some of the containers. Glue or duct tape the lids securely on the containers. Make sure the tops cannot be taken off.
- Sing songs or play music that the toddlers can accompany with their shakers and drums. Model for the toddlers how to keep rhythm with their instruments as they sing along and move to the music.

Extensions/Modifications

- Play recorded music from the toddlers' home cultures and encourage them to play along with their musical instruments.

Making Shadows

Area: Social Skills

Developmental Objectives

- to promote cognitive development
- to promote social development

Instructions

- Set up an area of the room where the toddlers can see their shadows. Set a large flashlight or desk lamp on a table pointing toward a blank wall in a dark corner of the classroom. Hang a white sheet or tape a large piece of white paper to the wall if you do not have a blank space. Show two toddlers how they can stand in front of the light and make shadows on the wall. For safety, make sure that the lamp cords are not where they will trip children and that the lamp does not get hot and burn them.
- Describe the shadows to the toddlers. Encourage them to use their bodies to make different kinds of shadows. For example, have them make a happy shadow or a sad shadow. Call the children by name as they make shadows.

Extensions/Modifications

- Change up the pairings of children so that they all have an opportunity to play with every other child in the classroom.
- On sunny days, encourage the toddlers to play shadow games outside. You could also quickly draw around a child's shadow with chalk as he stands on a sidewalk or concrete play area. Write his name by the shadow. Make a group of shadows together by drawing around the shadows of several children. Give the children pieces of chalk to draw on their shadows.

Learning to Relate to and Interact with the Environment

Digging in Wet Sand

Area: Classroom Community

Developmental Objectives

- to promote the development of gross- and fine-motor skills
- to promote social development

Instructions

- Digging in wet sand is a good way for toddlers to work alongside other toddlers and also have a sensory experience that helps build motor skills. On a warm day, add a bucket or more of water to the sandbox outside. Provide shovels for digging, containers for scooping and modeling, big dump trucks, and other sandbox toys.

- Encourage two or more toddlers to play with the sand and use parallel talk to describe what they are doing. See strategies for talking with toddlers on pages 26–27.
- Call each child by name and encourage social interactions.

Extensions/Modifications

- Add large dinosaurs, farm animals, and other animals to the sandbox play area. Encourage the toddlers to make animal sounds as they move the animals around and build landscapes.

Making Designs to Put on T-shirts

Area: Classroom Community

Developmental Objectives

- to promote the development of fine-motor skills
- to promote social development

Instructions

- Get several sets of fabric crayons from a local craft store. Peel the paper off the crayons and put them in a box. Give the toddlers large pieces of paper to scribble on with the fabric crayons. Show the toddlers how to use the long side of the crayon to make wide marks and the ends of the crayons to make narrow marks. Note that toddlers still put things in their mouths, so monitor them as they draw with the crayons.

- Write children's names on their drawings in pencil (not with the crayons since you will be using the drawings to make T-shirts).
- Ask each child to bring a T-shirt from home that has a plain front or back or buy inexpensive T-shirts and wash them before doing this project. Iron each toddler's drawing onto her T-shirt. Let the toddlers wear their shirts and take them home.

Extensions/Modifications

- Draw around the toddlers' hands with the fabric crayons and iron the drawings of their hands onto their T-shirts.
- Cut ten- to twelve-inch squares of fabric, one for each toddler, from a washed, plain, light-colored old sheet or other fabric. Trace the children's hands or have them draw on paper the size of the fabric squares. You can put children's names on the squares since they will not be wearing them. (Remember to write on the back and then trace on the front so the names will not be backward when you iron.) Iron the artwork onto the fabric squares, sew the squares together, and make a wall hanging, tablecloth, or curtain for the classroom.
- Make individual flags using the same technique above. Clip them to the playground fence with clothespins.

Building with Wood

Area: Classroom Community

Developmental Objectives

- to promote the development of gross- and fine-motor skills
- to promote cognitive development
- to promote social development

Instructions

- Collect pieces of scrap lumber from a local store that sells building materials or ask for permission to pick up scraps of wood from a construction site. Sand the ends and sides of each piece of wood so there are no rough edges or splinters. You'll need wood glue, empty containers such as tuna cans (make sure the edges aren't sharp), and stiff, short-handled brushes. Set up a construction area in the classroom or outdoors for the children to build and glue. Pour wood glue into the containers for the toddlers to use to attach pieces of wood with the brushes. Show the toddlers how to balance pieces of wood on top of other pieces and glue them together.

- Encourage the toddlers to build side by side and to talk with one another as they work. Use parallel talk to describe to a toddler what another child is doing. Model descriptive words, including sizes and shapes. See pages 26–27 for ways to talk with toddlers.

Extensions/Modifications

- Invite another class to visit and to see the sculptures. Encourage the toddlers to tell the visitors how they made their sculptures.
- Make a city from the sculptures by placing them on the floor and providing cars, trucks, and people for the toddlers' play.

- Write the children's names on their structures or on paper taped to the structures. Let the glued structures dry for a few days.
- Set up a painting area (either outside or inside) for the toddlers to paint their sculptures with water-soluble tempera paint. Have various colors and a variety of paintbrushes available for the toddlers to use.
- Display the sculptures around the room and talk with the toddlers about how they built them and the shapes, sizes, and colors of the pieces.

- Toddlers can take their sculptures home to keep and show their families.

Washing Dolls

Area: Classroom Community

Developmental Objectives

- to promote imaginative play
- to promote social development

Instructions

- Collect several baby dolls that can be put in water. Place a plastic pan on a low table and put a couple of inches of warm water in the pan. Have a clean sponge ready and a towel for drying. Put a plastic apron on a toddler and encourage him to wash the babies. Model for the child how to wash and dry the doll.

- Stay near and describe what the toddler is doing. Pretend for the doll and say aloud what the doll might be feeling as the toddler gives it a bath. Using feeling words, names of body parts, adjectives, and adverbs to describe how the toddler is bathing the doll.
- Have the toddlers wipe off the tables and hang up the towels when they are finished washing the babies.

Extensions/Modifications

- Place two dishpans on the table and encourage two toddlers to wash the dolls. Stay near and describe to each child what he is doing and what the other child is doing.

Take photographs of the toddlers washing the babies (as well as other play activities) to display at toddlers' eye level in the classroom.

Planting Vegetables

Area: Classroom Community

Developmental Objectives

- to promote the development of gross- and fine-motor skills
- to promote social development
- to promote cognitive development

Instructions

- Get large pots for plants or make a small raised garden on the playground. Fill the raised bed or pots with garden soil. Give the toddlers small shovels and rakes to spread out the dirt.
- Model for the toddlers how to drop seeds into the dirt or how to dig a hole and put in a potting plant. Plant herbs and vegetables such as basil, oregano, mint, cilantro, lettuce, spinach, squash, beans, peppers, and other plants that grow well in your area.
- Model for the toddlers how to water the plants with a watering can or hose.
- When the plants are big enough to eat, show the toddlers how the plants can be used as food. Wash them and use them for snacks and for toddlers' meals, or send some of the herbs and vegetables home with the toddlers.

Extensions/Modifications

- Visit a community garden, if one is close, and ask to have a plot for the classroom or school. Walk to the garden and explore, and involve toddlers and their families in growing vegetables for their home use.
- Visit a farmers' market and let the toddlers look at all of the foods for sale. Talk with them about the foods.
- Ask a local farmer to visit the classroom and to bring different vegetables for the toddlers to see and explore. Use some of the vegetables for snacktime that day.

Putting Toys Away

Area: Classroom Community

Developmental Objectives

- to promote cognitive development
- to promote social development

Instructions

- Arrange the classroom so it is easy for the children to get toys and other things and to put them away. Have pegs for toddlers to hang things on; low, sturdy shelves; and baskets, boxes, and plastic bins where toys and other things are kept.
- Take photographs of toys, print and laminate them, and tape them onto shelves and bins to show toddlers where items belong. Model for the toddlers where things go and how to put things away when they are finished playing with or using them.
- Make a picture book of the classroom toys on the shelves and in bins or containers. Look at the book with the toddlers and talk about the toys and where they are kept.

Extensions/Modifications

- Model cooperation by doing what it is you want toddlers to do, including helping others, and saying it aloud. "Pick up that book and put it here." Your attitude and approach sets the stage for toddlers' helping behaviors and cooperation. They want to help, so make it easy and acceptable for them to do so. Do not expect perfection. Remember that this is a learning experience.

Going for a Nature Walk

Area: Broader Community and Society

Developmental Objectives

- to promote the development of gross-motor skills
- to promote social development
- to promote cognitive development

Instructions

- Take a nature walk with the children. Take photographs of each part of the walk, beginning with toddlers putting on their coats, then going out the door, walking on the sidewalk, stopping to look at things, talking with one another and their caregivers, and so on.

- As you walk, stop and look at trees, the sky, flowers, plants, and animals, such as squirrels and insects. Teach the toddlers not to pick wildflowers or flowers people have planted in landscapes. Talk with them about the flowers and other things they see, describing colors, shapes, smells, sizes, and locations.

Extensions/Modifications

- Print the photographs and label and laminate them. Make a wall display at toddlers' eye level by putting the photographs in sequence, showing the walk from beginning to end.
- Talk with the toddlers about the nature walk. Ask them what they did first, what they did they next, and so on. Describe the photographs and encourage the toddlers to point to and talk about the pictures as they remember what they did and when.
- Make a picture book from the photographs for the toddlers to look at and talk about.

Collecting Rocks, Leaves, and Twigs

Area: Broader Community and Society

Developmental Objectives

- to promote the development of gross- and fine-motor skills
- to promote cognitive development
- to promote social development

Instructions

- Take a nature walk outside with the toddlers. Give each toddler a clear plastic bag to collect small rocks, leaves, or other objects found in nature. Write each toddler's name on his bag with a permanent marker.
- As you walk, talk with the toddlers about the things they see. See pages 26–27 for ideas on how to talk with the children during and after the walk. Encourage each toddler to add a few things to his bag.
- Back in the classroom, tape the bags of found nature objects on the wall or on a large display board at toddlers' eye level.

Extensions/Modifications

- Create a classroom nature area where toddlers can explore the items they have found. Invite each toddler to take one thing from his bag to share with the class. Make sure that all items are safe and that none present a choking hazard.

People in Our School

Area: Broader Community and Society

Developmental Objectives

- to promote the development of gross-motor skills
- to promote cognitive development
- to promote social development

Instructions

- Take the toddlers on a walk through the building and around it. Take photographs of the people who work in and around the building during the walk. Talk with the toddlers about the room or place where each person works and the type of work she does.
- Print and laminate the photographs to make a picture book for the toddlers.
- Talk with the toddlers about the people who work in the school or program community. Repeat what each person does and explain how everyone helps make the program what it is.

Extensions/Modifications

- Put the photo books where toddlers can access them. Make additional books and rotate them in the toddlers' play area.

Fire Trucks and Firefighters

Area: Broader Community and Society

Developmental Objectives

- to promote cognitive development
- to promote social development
- to promote health and safety

Instructions

- Toddlers may be afraid of police and firefighters because of the imposing way they look. Invite the local fire department to bring their truck to the school and park it where the toddlers can see it. Invite one or two of the firefighters to show the toddlers their masks and suits. Help the toddlers feel comfortable looking at and interacting with the firefighters.
- Take photographs of the fire truck and firefighters interacting with the toddlers. Make a collage or display of the photographs.

- Make a picture book of the photographs.
- When houses are on fire, toddlers may hide or be afraid of the firefighters who come into the house to get them. Teach the toddlers that firefighters come to their houses to help them if there is a fire.
- Have toy fire trucks, fire helmets, and small hoses for toddlers to pretend to be firefighters.

Extensions/Modifications

- Ask firefighters to provide families with information about how to get free fire alarms installed in their homes. Make a display at the entrance of the school with the information where families will see it.
- Ask firefighters to present a program on fire safety and invite families.

Exploring the Community

Area: Broader Community and Society

Developmental Objectives

- to promote the development of gross-motor skills
- to promote social development
- to promote cognitive development

Instructions

- Take walks to places that are close, such as parks, community gardens, and libraries, or just around the block to look at different buildings and to see different things. Watching a building being torn down or a new one being built is very interesting. Just make sure that it is safe and that there are no health risks or hazards in watching. Take photographs of the toddlers as they have these experiences and print, laminate, and label them.
- Make a wall collage of each of the places you visit and talk with the toddlers about what they saw and did. Use the ideas on pages 26–27 for talking with the toddlers. Learn common words and phrases in children's home languages and use them as you talk with the toddlers.

Extensions/Modifications

- Create picture books or photo albums of each place you visited. Put the albums in the play area for the toddlers to look at, remember, and talk about their experiences.

References

Bronfenbrenner, Urie. 1979. *The Ecology of Human Development*. Cambridge, MA: Harvard University Press.

———. 1994. "Ecological Models of Human Development." In *The International Encyclopedia of Education*. 2nd ed. Vol. 3, edited by Torsten Husén and T. Neville Postlethwaite, 1643–1647. New York: Elsevier Science.

Bronfenbrenner, Urie, and Pamela Morris. 1998. "The Ecology of Developmental Processes." In *Handbook of Child Psychology*. 5th ed. Edited by William Damon. Vol. 1: *Theoretical Models of Human Development,* edited by Richard M. Lerner, 993–1028. New York: John Wiley & Sons.

CECMHC (Center for Early Childhood Mental Health Consultation). 2008. "Infant Toddler Temperament Tool (IT³)." www.ecmhc.org/temperament.

Hoefle, Vicki. 2015. "The Difference between Praise and Encouragement." PBS Parents. www.pbs.org/parents/expert-tips-advice/2015/05/difference -praise-encouragement-matters.

Mid-State Early Childhood Direction Center. 2012. *Developmental Checklists: Birth to Five*. Syracuse, NY: Early Childhood Direction Center. http:// ecdc.syr.edu/wp-content/uploads/2013/01/Developmental_checklists _Updated2012.pdf.

NAEYC (National Association for the Education of Young Children). 2009. *NAEYC Standards for Early Childhood Professional Preparation Programs*. Washington, DC: NAEYC. www.naeyc.org/files/naeyc/file/positions /ProfPrepStandards09.pdf.

———. 2013. "'Good Job' Alternatives." *Teaching Young Children* 7 (1): 6–7. www.naeyc.org/tyc/files/tyc/%22Good%20Job%22%20Alternatives.pdf.

———. 2016. *Overview of the 10 NAEYC Early Learning Standards*. Washington, DC: NAEYC. www.naeyc.org/academy/files/academy/OverviewStandards .pdf.

US Department of Health and Human Services/Administration for Children and Families. 2016. *Milestones Checklists*. In English and Spanish. Atlanta, GA: Centers for Disease Control and Prevention. www.cdc.gov/ncbddd /actearly/pdf/parents_pdfs/MilestonesChecklists.pdf.